THE DARING EXPLOITS

OF

PIRATE BLACK SAM BELLAMY

From Cape Cod to the Caribbean

JAMIE L.H. GOODALL

THE
History
PRESS

Published by The History Press
Charleston, SC
www.historypress.com

First published 2023

Manufactured in the United States

ISBN 9781467151207

Library of Congress Control Number: 2023932168

My answer to the magnificent Jennifer Opal who once asked on Twitter:

"Anyone else with ADHD doing something they shouldn't be doing right now to distract themselves from important work they should be doing but thinking about it overwhelms you?"

Yes. Unequivocally yes.

CONTENTS

Acknowledgements   9
Prologue   11

PART I. THE VILLAIN'S ORIGIN STORY
1. The Mysterious Origins of Samuel Bellamy   15
  Black Sam at Plymouth   17
2. New England's Piratical Origins   21
  Queen Elizabeth and Hawkins   24
  The Price of Peace   26
  A Tale of Two Plymouths   28
  Pirates and Religion   31
  King James and Unrest   32

PART II. THE BUCCANEERS TAKE THE SEA (CIRCA 1650–1689)
3. Imperial Growing Pains   37
  Mess with the Bull, Get the Horns   38
  The (Alleged) Adulterous Cannibal Pirate   40
  War and Profit   42
4. The Protectorate, the Restoration, and the
  Glorious Revolution   49
  What Cannot Defend Itself Shall Not Be Defended   50
  The Pirates Find a Refuge   52

From Port Royal to Boston: A Heavenly Match 53

An Englishman, a Dutchman, and a *Flying Horse* 55

The Navigation Acts 60

Be Well to Portsmouth, and Let Not Poor Nelly Starve 63

PART III. THE PIRATE ROUND (CIRCA 1690–1714)

5. The Nine Years' War (1688–1697) 69

King William's War: The North American Theater 69

Thomas Tew, the Rhode Island Pirate 72

6. The War of the Spanish Succession (1701–1715) 79

Queen Anne's War: The North American Theater 81

John Quelch Goes Rogue 81

A Man with a Plan 84

Death Is Great for the Appetite 87

**PART IV. DAMN THEM FOR A PACK OF CRAFTY RASCALS:
BELLAMY ENTERS THE CHAT**

7. The Early Trials and Tribulations of Black Sam 93

Love, Lust, or Legend? 93

You've Got a Friend in Me 96

No Honor Among Thieves 98

Robin Hood Meets the Flying Gang 102

The Fairly Odd Couple 103

8. The Curse of the *Whydah* 106

Going Quick Down into Hell 107

Bellamy and Captain Beer 108

Waves Crack with Wicked Fury 110

Bellamy Gets Wrecked 115

Mooncussers versus Cyprian Southack 116

The Enemy of Mankind's Long and Sad Walk to
the Tree of Death 117

**PART V. THE LIFE OF THE DEAD IS PLACED IN THE MEMORY
OF THE LIVING**

**9. Death Is Just Another Path: The Legacy of Black Sam Bellamy
and the End of Golden Age Pirates** 123

The Witch of Wellfleet 125

Bellamy, Maria, and Aesop's Tables 126

CONTENTS

Glossary   129
Notes   133
Bibliography   149
Index   157
About the Author   159

ACKNOWLEDGEMENTS

If you had told teenage me that I would one day be the proud author of not one, not two, but *three* published books, I probably would have rolled my eyes so far back in my head they got stuck (that's how that works, right, Momma?). Who knew a girl from a working-class family who grew up in rural North Carolina could go so far? (Props to my AP English teacher, Mr. Donald Lourcey, for being one of the believers without whom college would have remained a distant dream!)

I'm grateful to Mike Kinsella and the team at The History Press—from the copyeditors to the production staff, the designers to the marketing crew—for bringing my work to life yet again. And many thanks to the Library of Congress, the New York Public Library, and Wikimedia Commons for not only providing an extensive array of open-access images and artwork but also making them easily accessible. Without your efforts, there would be no images within these pages.

I'd like to extend a special thanks to those whose constructive criticism of my past works has made me a (hopefully) better researcher and writer. In particular, without Cindy Vallar's review of *Pirates of the Chesapeake Bay* in which she highlighted my use of a bad archival source (thus providing an inaccurate account of Samuel Bellamy and the wreck of the *Whydah*), this book would not exist. Special thanks goes to Kenneth J. Kinkor for his invaluable work on *The Whydah Sourcebook* (and to Eric Jay Dolin for his willingness to share it with me). Props to my Pirate Queen twin, Rebecca Simon, for her never-ending support and for working with me to create space in the pirate world for badass women studying piracy and the maritime world in its various forms (like our friends and colleagues Nush Powell, Elaine Murphy, Jo Esra, Casey Schmitt, Hannah Farber, Claire Jowitt, Sue Jones, and SO MANY others)!

As always, my love and eternal gratitude go out to the people who love me well: Amanda, Rob, Luke, Kerry, Heather, Sarah, Sam, Ashley, Kayleabug, Jen, Zacktober, Charlie, Jonathan, Katie, Ben Keely, Kelsa, Michael, Will, Tripp, Calley, Chris, Naomi, Matty, Kelsey, Leah, and Ryan. Same goes for my amazing family: Momma (Kim); Daddy (Darren); my brothers Tyler and Kenneth; Grandma and Papa (Shirley Jean, and Pat); Dad (Steve); Mum (Susan); Granny Brown; my sisters Joanna, Kathryn, and Eileen; Danny and Elizabeth, my niblings; my aunts; and my uncles. This list is far from exhaustive, so if your name does not appear, please forgive me. I blame my exhausted brain and ADHD-affected memory.

Last, but never least, much love to Kyle. You're my person…you make me brave. Saying "I love you" just can't encapsulate what you mean to me. Thank you. And to my loves, lil baby JT and old man TJ, thank you for making me the mother I would never have been otherwise. Between JT's sleepy tongue and TJ's epic diva side-eye, you bring me immense joy.

And to all my supporters near and far: you rock!

P.S. To my new friend Sean…Mikey…Samwise Gamgee…Ready to make that Black Sam Bellamy biopic?

PROLOGUE

The only use and advantage of the American colonies… [is] *the monopoly of their consumption, and the carriage of their produce.*
—*John Baker Holroyd, First Earl of Sheffield*[1]

At the dawn of the golden age of piracy in the mid-seventeenth century, piracy was hardly a new or radical phenomenon. One of the earliest records documenting piracy is an inscription from Egyptian pharaoh Amenhotep III (1390–1353 BCE), in which he describes how he established defenses along the Nile Delta to protect the Egyptian kingdom from ruthless commerce raiders. And the European rulers of the seventeenth and eighteenth centuries were far from the first to issue laws to try to eradicate piracy. When pirates pillaged and plundered the ancient Roman town of Ostia Antica, the Roman Senate passed the *lex Gabinia*. The law gave Roman general Pompey the Great proconsular powers in any province located within fifty miles of the Mediterranean Sea without being an elected magistrate, with the express purpose of eradicating piracy. For centuries, pirates and privateers were used as convenient and effective weapons in the arsenals of competing empires. And they were quickly discarded once they had outlived their usefulness.

My purpose here is twofold: to provide as detailed an account as available historical evidence makes possible of the rise and fall of Samuel "Black Sam" Bellamy and to highlight the importance of piracy and privateering to the region of colonial New England. The history presented within these pages is hardly exhaustive. Many thousands of pirates and privateers operated between the mid-seventeenth and mid-eighteenth centuries. Historian Marcus Rediker estimated that nearly four thousand pirates operated between 1716 and 1726 alone![2] So, if I have failed to include your favorite New England pirate story or Sam Bellamy fun fact, please forgive me. In the bibliography you will find other books related to this era of piracy, several dedicated specifically to Bellamy, the *Whydah*, and New England to help satisfy your curiosity. For now, let's enter the wild, mysterious, and complex world of the golden age pirates.

Note: This book contains many excerpts from primary sources that contain misspellings. In order to preserve the sources' authenticity, these errors remain. All dates given are, to the best of the author's knowledge, according to the Julian calendar, as England/Great Britain did not adopt the Gregorian calendar until the passage of the Calendar (New Style) Act in 1750. There are most certainly instances where the author has mistakenly used the New Style instead of the Old Style. For a detailed explanation of the switch from using the Julian (Old Style) calendar to the Gregorian (New Style) calendar between the late sixteenth and early twentieth centuries, see C.R. Cheney and Michael Jones, eds., A Handbook of Dates: For Students of English History, *4ᵗʰ ed. (Cambridge, UK: Cambridge University Press, 2000).*

PART I

THE VILLAIN'S ORIGIN STORY

Chapter 1

THE MYSTERIOUS ORIGINS
OF SAMUEL BELLAMY

All sins have their origins in a sense of inferiority, otherwise called ambition.
—Cesare Pavese[3]

What is a beginning but an end enduring? When pirate Samuel "Black Sam" Bellamy perished during a wicked nor'easter off the coast of Cape Cod in April 1717, British officials believed this "agreable news" put a definitive end to Bellamy's story.[4] No one could foresee that the discovery of Bellamy's wrecked ship, *Whydah*, over two centuries later would breathe new life into his story. During a Thanksgiving dinner party in 1981, Barry Clifford regaled guests with the story of Bellamy and his alleged love affair with a young girl from the Cape named Maria Hallett. After he concluded the story, Clifford was faced with a challenging question from one of the guests. Walter Cronkite (yes, *the* Walter Cronkite) asked Clifford: "You said that you are interested in looking for the *Whydah*; why don't you do it?" After a split-second assessment of his life, Clifford realized that he was tired of "living a life of quiet desperation." In that moment, Clifford decided to turn his passion for maritime exploration and fascination with Bellamy into a quest to "dig up a piece of the past and make an impact on history."[5]

But who was this Samuel Bellamy whose exploits left an indelible mark on the history of golden age piracy? There are no conclusive records of Bellamy's life before 1716. Historian Kenneth J. Kinkor has tried to parse Bellamy's identity through a combination of genealogical and archival research. One issue facing researchers has been whether "Samuel" was his

William Dummer, lieutenant governor of Massachusetts (1716–30), portrait by Frederic Porter Vinton, 1886. *Wikimedia Commons*.

real first name. Contemporary chronicler of pirate tales Captain Charles Johnson does not use Bellamy's first name in his section on Captain Bellamy and the *Whydah* in volume 2 of *The History of the Pyrates*. But Johnson does reference a Captain **Charles** Bellamy in volume 1 of *A General History of the Pyrates*. In his description of an alleged "general council" meeting of pirate captains regarding King George I's September 1717 proclamation for suppressing pirates, Johnson lists "Charles Bellamy" immediately after "Paul Williams," the known partner in crime of Samuel Bellamy. According to Kinkor, if Johnson knew the captain of the *Whydah* to be Charles Bellamy, then Johnson's record of this meeting's attendees is dubious since Bellamy presumably died prior to this council being convened. But if Johnson believed the *Whydah*'s captain to be Samuel Bellamy, this would suggest that there were two pirate captains with the surname Bellamy operating at the same time. Although there is a Charles Bellamy listed among the signatories of a 1724 petition requesting protection along Maine's frontier during Dummer's War, there is no documentation connecting him with acts of piracy. Given that no corroborating evidence has been found to support the existence of a pirate captain named Charles Bellamy, this possibility is equally suspect.[6]

But Johnson's work is not the sole account of pirate Samuel Bellamy's origins. There are a few different reports of Bellamy's background in archival sources. In the 1716 deposition of Abijah Savage, captain of the *Bonetta* of Antigua, Savage recalled that while being held prisoner, he was told that the commander of the pirate sloop *Mary Anne* was "one Samuel Bellamy who declared himself to be an Englishman born in London."[7] Kinkor identified two individuals named Samuel Bellamy of appropriate age born in London who could be the pirate captain. The first was the son of John and Ann Bellamy, baptized on December 12, 1673. The second was born to Samuel and Elizabeth "Bellamee," baptized on June 27, 1690. Other evidence points to Captain Bellamy being from England's West Country.[8] In the May 3, 1717 publication of the *Rhode Island Dispatch*, an article recounts the experience of Captain Beer, whose vessel was taken and plundered by Bellamy and his crew at the beginning of April. According to Captain Beer, he believed Bellamy to be "born in the West of England."[9] Further, Andrew Turbett and Robert Gilmore, crew members of the vessel *Agnes* seized by Bellamy shortly after, deposed that while they were held captive aboard the *Whydah*, they were informed that the vessel's captain was Samuel Bellamy, "an Englishman born in Plymouth and said to have a wife and family in or near Canterbury."[10] There were several Bellamy families in the villages of Hittisleigh and Drewsteignton near Plymouth in the eighteenth century. Taken together, the evidence suggests that "Samuell" Bellamy, son of tenant farmers Stephen and Elizabeth Pain Bellamy of Devonshire, may be the most likely candidate for being Black Sam. Elizabeth Bellamy died in late February 1689 either while giving birth to Samuel or shortly thereafter due to complications. Samuel, her sixth child, was baptized on March 18, just a few weeks after her burial.[11]

BLACK SAM AT PLYMOUTH

The narrative of the pirate Black Sam Bellamy that follows is rooted in the belief that the son born to Stephen and Elizabeth Pain Bellamy is the legendary "Prince of Pirates." In the late eighteenth century, Hittisleigh was a hilly region of scattered farms. Incomes were modest as the soil was largely clay, which made plowing difficult and caused drainage problems. Despite the soil being generally barren and unsuitable for livestock, the local farmers were able to produce wheat, barley, and potatoes. Bellamy was born into this context of growing social unrest and economic upheaval. At that time, half the nation teetered on the brink of devastation. Most of those who were one misstep away from dying of starvation lived in rural communities.[12] By the time of Bellamy's birth, there had already been an exodus of young English men and women seeking work in England's cities and ports or taking their chances in one of England's overseas colonies. As his father's only living son, Bellamy was the heir apparent of the family estate. With the average male agricultural laborer earning less than twenty pounds per year, Bellamy was not likely to inherit much.[13] Scholars have posited that, after Elizabeth's death and struggling to make ends meet, Stephen Bellamy relocated the family to the coastal town of Plymouth, where he could take a factory job.

Samuel Bellamy's time in Plymouth was presumably instructive. The West Country had a storied reputation as a hotbed of piracy. Lord High Admiral Charles Howard once remarked that there were so many men in the West Country involved in piracy that the region's fishing vessels "must have been 'manned' by women."[14] Similarly, Charles Kingsford, expert on the history of fifteenth-century England, referred to piracy in the West Country as "the School of English Seamen."[15] Both fishermen and the gentry benefited from the supplemental income that the plunder from their economy of opportunity provided. To further increase their domination of the fishing industry, West Country residents invested the financial gains from their plunder back into their fishing enterprises.[16] Additionally, many of the most prominent Elizabethan "sea dogs"—privateers commissioned by Queen Elizabeth I—were born and raised in England's West Country. The nation relied heavily on these West Countrymen, such as Sirs Francis Drake, John Hawkins, Walter Raleigh, Humphrey Gilbert, and Richard Grenville, to defend England against invasion during a period of incessant warfare. The fact that they filled the royal coffers and gentry pockets didn't hurt either.

Bellamy would no doubt have been immersed particularly in the stories of Sir Francis Drake, hero of Plymouth. When he was quite young, Drake was placed into the care of his relative William Hawkins, a skilled sea captain and prolific trader of enslaved Africans. Drake was tutored in the navigational arts and quickly learned how the powerful Plymouth gentry profited from all manner of maritime violence.[17] He used his knowledge and skills to his advantage, taking the capital from his early voyages to purchase property throughout Devonshire. As a result, Drake became one of the most influential landed gentry in the county. This afforded him the opportunity to serve in a number of important positions, including

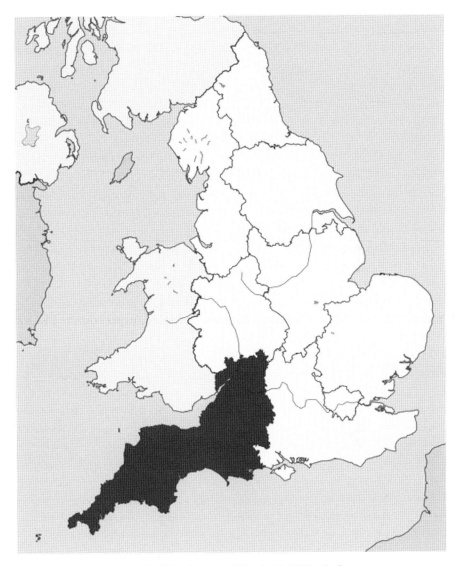

A digital map highlighting the West Country of England. *Wikimedia Commons.*

mayor of Plymouth, a member of Parliament, and deputy lord lieutenant of Devonshire.[18]

The influence of the Elizabethan sea dogs on Plymouth would be felt among the city's mariners, like Samuel Bellamy, for generations. Given the success Bellamy had during his short-lived pirate career, his unofficial maritime education was undoubtedly informed by these sea marauders.

19

Some believe Bellamy's seafaring skills were also developed while serving aboard a merchantman or naval ship during the War of the Spanish Succession (1701–14). Since he had just turned thirteen when the war broke out, it is unclear whether Bellamy entered service willingly or was the victim of a practice called impressment.[19] When the war ended, Bellamy was in his mid-twenties and, like so many others, suddenly out of a job.[20] So, he became one of the hundreds of thousands of English emigrants who hoped to achieve economic security in the colonies of North America. His arrival would prove fortuitous. The third period of the golden age of piracy, host to the "worst of these pirate excesses," was about to begin.[21] But why did the West Country develop a penchant for piracy and how did this influence the burgeoning New England colonies over three thousand miles away?

Chapter 2
NEW ENGLAND'S PIRATICAL ORIGINS

There is a propensity in man to take pleasure in the sight or relation of human sin and suffering...This curiosity [is] *a depraved appetite...* [that] *is almost universal and therefore natural.*
—Henry St. Clair [22]

In the early seventeenth century, the English, Dutch, and French each tried to establish permanent settlements in the region of North America that would become New England. But most of these colonies were short-lived. It wasn't until the Pilgrims, a group of Puritans fleeing religious persecution, established Plymouth Colony in 1620 that the English created a permanent presence in the area. Two years later, the Plymouth Council granted a patent establishing the Province of Maine to Sir Ferdinando Gorges and John Mason. Despite the hardships these early settlers faced, publications like John Smith's *A Description of New England* (1616) and the accounts of Edward Winslow and William Bradford in *Mourt's Relation* (1622) encouraged other Puritans to immigrate to this "New World." Between 1620 and 1640, a period known as the Great Migration, an estimated twenty thousand people left England to settle in New England, setting up three additional colonies and one new province. In 1630, Puritans founded the Massachusetts Bay Colony while John Mason split from Sir Gorges to carve out the Province of New Hampshire. The other two colonies were established in 1636. One, the Colony of Rhode Island and Providence Plantations, was founded by Roger Williams, who had been banished from Massachusetts Bay. The other was

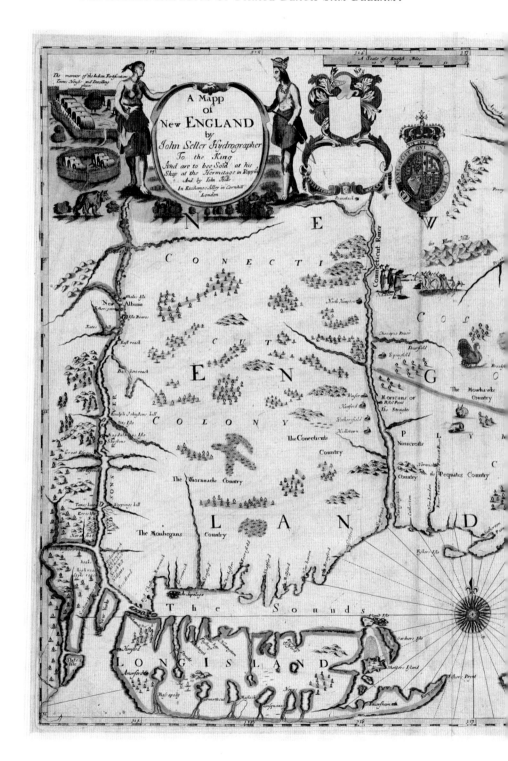

A map of New England,
by John Seller, 1675.
*Courtesy of the Mapping
Boston Collection—Norman B.
Leventhal Map & Education
Center, Boston Public Library.*

the Connecticut Colony, originally organized as a settlement for a Puritan congregation. To understand colonial New England's socioeconomic development and the region's relationship with piracy, it's important to grasp the broader political impact of England's transition from the Tudor Dynasty to the Stuart Dynasty on its colonization efforts.

Queen Elizabeth and Hawkins

Queen Elizabeth I (1558–1603) was famous for using privateers to her advantage during the wars and conflicts that encompassed over half her reign. These sea dogs, with their privileged pedigrees, had long enjoyed the perks of crown support and the admiration of many English men and women who viewed their borderline piracies as a patriotic service to the nation. In the waning years of Queen Elizabeth I's reign, there was a radical shift in how residents of the West Country approached their economic future. The time of the sea dogs was ending. But not everyone had gotten the memo. In 1594, Richard Hawkins, son of sea dog Sir John Hawkins and a privateer in his own right, had recently plundered the town of Valparaiso in Chile while on commission to "explore." His true intention, however, was to build on his father's legacy and do as much damage to the Spanish as he could. While leaving the scene of his pillaging, Hawkins found himself engaged in a three-day battle off the Chilean coast against two Spanish galleons sent to apprehend him. Surveying the damage to his ship, Hawkins noted that the ship's sails were torn, the masts and pumps were shattered, and there was over seven feet of water in the hold. Much of his crew had been killed in the melee while those who survived were badly "hurt, and in a manner altogether fruiteles."[23] One of the Spanish commanders, Don Beltrán de Castro, promised Hawkins that if the Englishmen surrendered, he would receive them *a buena guerra* and give them "life and libertie" by returning them to England.[24] The men, reeling from their wounds and afraid of drowning in their sinking ship, agreed. They were brought to Lima to recover while Don Castro made his case for returning the prisoners to England.

Nobody expects the Spanish Inquisition, but Hawkins sure wished he had. For the next few years, Don Castro became locked in a legal battle with the Inquisition, which oversaw more than just religious crimes. The Inquisition firmly believed that Hawkins and his men were pirates who should be sent to Spain to face judgment. Unfortunately for Hawkins, the

The Burning Ship, by Howard Pyle, 1898. *Wikimedia Commons*.

Inquisition prevailed, and the men were transferred to a prison in Seville in late 1597. After a failed escape attempt, Hawkins was kept in "irons day and night…in the common jail amongst murderers, rogues, and thieves."[25] In a letter to Queen Elizabeth I, dated June 12, 1598, Hawkins wrote of the "manifold miseries and grievous calamities" he and his men had endured while imprisoned. He entreated her to "strike while the iron is hot" so that the "merciless, faithless, filthy and most barbarous" Spanish may be destroyed.[26] A few months later, Hawkins wrote to the Earl of Essex, begging him to impart to Queen Elizabeth I that "in recompence of my so long and faithful service, with that of my deceased father, I may be redeemed out of this miserable and tyrannical imprisonment."[27] Finally, after countless letters to the queen and many prominent government officials, Hawkins's letter of June 1602 to Sir Robert Cecil brought his eight-year suffering to an end. After receiving a ransom payment of £3,000, the Spanish released Hawkins, and he returned to Plymouth to resume his former life. Shortly after his return, Queen Elizabeth I died, taking the crown's support of the sea dogs with her. Hawkins expected that he would be able to continue antagonizing the Spanish without reprisal, especially after he was elected mayor of Plymouth and knighted by King James I. Soon, Hawkins was appointed to represent Plymouth in Parliament and to serve as vice-admiral of Devon.

The Price of Peace

When Elizabeth I died in 1603, she was without an heir, and the fate of the sea dogs was left hanging in the balance. In her final years, a number of English politicians, including Sir Robert Cecil, had worked to establish a plan of succession that would not arouse civil unrest. So it was that King James I (1603–1625), Elizabeth I's nearest royal relative, ascended to the English throne.[28] James I, recognizing the significant debt the English government was in as a result of the Elizabethan wars, departed from his predecessor's proclivity for commerce raiding. Instead, James I decided to approach foreign policy from a position of peace upon his ascension to the throne. So, what would become of Elizabeth I's sea dogs and their benefactors?

Those engaged in privateering, piracy, and other means of illicit commerce did not have to wait long to discover their fate. Peace meant that James I no longer had need for the men-of-war and privateers of yesteryear, so he rescinded all letters of marque. Various diplomats warned James I that a sudden increase in unemployment among those in the maritime industry could result in a rapid turn toward outright piracy. For example, Venetian diplomat Giovanni Carlo Scaramelli informed the king about a couple of recent acts of piracy against the Republic of Venice. First, Englishmen Christopher Olororeh and Nicholas Alvel had plundered the *Geopandita* in the Ionian Sea as it traveled from Smyrna to Venice. The cargo was worth "upwards of a hundred thousand ducats." Around the same time, in the same sea, an Englishman named Captain Tompkins had seized the *Balbiana*, taking "about three hundred thousand ducats in cash, cloth of gold, silk, and wool" before sinking the vessel with its crew still on board "so as to conceal his crime." As such, the Doge of Venice sought "restitution of the booty, part of which was in the hands of the Lord Admiral." According to Scaramelli, the king listened "with extreme impatience, twisting his body, striking his hands together, and tapping with his feet…and said in a loud voice, 'By God I'll hang the pirates with my own hands, and my Lord Admiral as well.'" Sir Robert Cecil, the secretary of state of England, reportedly replied that these "pirates" were those who had taken to "buccaneering under the late Queen."[29]

King James I took action immediately, issuing his first proclamation against piracy on September 30, 1603. The king, "informed, through the manifold and daily complaints made by his own subjects and by others, of continual piracies and depredations," issued several orders. Any captain, mariner, owner, or victualler of any vessel that was convicted of committing "piracy, depredation, or 'murther at the sea upon any of his Majesties friends,'" as well as anyone who seized "any goods belonging to subjects of allies," would be summarily put to death. The sentence was final and could not be appealed. His Majesty's subjects were thus forbidden from "aiding or receiving any 'Pirat or sea rover.'" Every quarter, vice-admirals were required to certify with the Court of Admiralty all "men-of-warre" that had "put to sea, or returned home with goods taken at sea." Anyone who violated this order would be fined forty pounds for each infraction. Lastly, to prevent future collusion with pirates, vice-admirals and officers were not to let any ship go to sea without being inspected "to see whether she is furnished for the wars and not for fishing or trade." If there was any suspicion about the intentions of those on board the vessel, "good surety shall be exacted before they let the ship sail." Therefore, if an officer gave license to a ship, the officer would have to "answer for such piracies as may be committed by those" aboard that ship.[30]

Less than a decade later, "having [again] bene informed through the manifolde complaints made" about the proliferation of piracy, King James I issued another proclamation. Not only did the king "reiterate and inculcate his loathing and detestation" of such crimes, but he also noted "that most of these great faults are continued by the connivence, or corruption in many the subordinate Officers, especially such as are resident in and neere the Ports and Maritine Counties." The proclamation reaffirmed that any person convicted of piracy would subsequently "suffer death, with confiscation of lands and goods," and that anyone who was caught "furnishing, Victualing, ayding, receiving, relieving, comforting or abetting, any Pirate or Sea-rover" would also be executed. Officers were to immediately apprehend any suspected pirates and their accomplices, holding them without bail to await trial. James I hoped that this time these punishments would be taken more seriously and serve as a warning to all what the consequences were not just for committing piracy but also for supporting such "enormious malefactors" in any way.[31] King James I's attitude toward piracy had a ripple effect, pushing the pirates toward Caribbean and North American colonies, far from the eyes of the crown.

A Tale of Two Plymouths

As mentioned previously, King James I recognized how costly the Elizabethan wars had been. Similarly, King Philip III of Spain, who inherited the war from *his* predecessor, understood Spain's precarious position since the treasuries were exhausted. Between late 1603 and early 1604, the two monarchs were deep in peace negotiations, which offended Hawkins's sensibilities. He urged the commissioners in charge of the peace talks to demand compensation from Spain for his prior imprisonment. Those demands went unheeded, which many believe prompted Hawkins to turn his attention to reestablishing Plymouth's former reputation as a formidable maritime foe and build his own fortune. For example, in November 1603, Hawkins released suspected pirate Josias Goodwyn after receiving forty or fifty pounds in gold from him, and the following year, alleged pirate Captain Fall offered Hawkins his ship in return for dropping charges against him. Others reported that Hawkins received bribes in the form of gold from one pirate and silk from another, and he routinely released suspected pirates.[32]

But as foreign merchants increasingly complained about losses they sustained due to Hawkins's behavior, he came under unwanted scrutiny. When French shipowner Jean Guerrin sought justice for the loss of his ship in October 1603, the Privy Council granted him an order for the arrest of the culprit, William Hull. Guerrin brought the order of arrest to Hawkins, who failed to act on it, probably because he had acknowledged the ship as a legitimate prize upon accepting a bribe of more than £500 from Hull. Not long after Guerrin's case, a merchant from Normandy named Guillaume Bouillon complained that he had been robbed by the nefarious pirate Thomas Pin, who was able to fence the pilfered goods in Plymouth. Bouillon also learned that the pirates who attacked him had been "armed and victualled a little before in the port of Plymouth in England" by Hawkins. Hoping to have his goods returned to him, or to receive some sort of compensation, Bouillon demanded from Hawkins "the restitution of part of the merchandise as he had it in his possession." When Hawkins offered Bouillon an offensively small return of his goods, Bouillon went to the council in London, where he received a commission to "apprehend the pirates and those who had bought and concealed the said merchandise." When Bouillon returned to Plymouth to fulfill his commission, he found one of the pirates and their victualler in Hawkins's own home. After apprehending the criminals, Hawkins was so angered that he disregarded the council's commission to Bouillon and freed the men so that they could unload and transport the remaining stolen goods. Exasperated, the merchant sought help from the mayor of Plymouth, to no avail. Bouillon found that both Hawkins and the mayor of Plymouth had made themselves "accomplice[s]" of these evil designs" and that they "converted to their own use" the commodities "having compounded with those who had bought and concealed the said merchandise."[33]

Enclosed with Bouillon's petition was more incriminating evidence against Hawkins. In a short list of other French ships recently plundered and taken to various English ports, nearly half were brought to Plymouth. For example, pirates took Estienne Berault's ship to Plymouth, where it was "seized by the Vice-Admiral of that place without having arrested the pirates." Then there were the vessels of Pierre Bottins and Jehan Basset, both of which were "taken and plundered by pirates" who "came to an anchor at the entrance of Plymouth, where the Vice-Admiral and the secretary of the Admiral" took a share of the stolen goods and sold them for personal profit. Two barks from Saint-Jean-de-Luz laden with wool were "carried off to the entrance of Plymouth, where the said wool was unloaded"; a bark from Marennes carrying Spanish wine and gold was plundered in the "harbour of Plymouth

Blind justice holding sword and scales, seven men on gallows in background, British warship and pirate ship in close combat below, frontispiece from *The History and Lives of All the Most Notorious Pirates, and Their Crews* by Captain Charles Johnson, 1725. *Courtesy of the Library of Congress.*

and under the protection both of the town and the castle"; and a bark from Granville was "taken and boarded at the entrance to Plymouth, where the pirates were anchored." The pirates then "killed the principal merchant and threw him into the sea" after they pilfered the vessel. Afterward, "the pirates returned to anchor at the place from which they started and sold the merchandise."[34]

When these damning allegations against Hawkins were brought to Lord Admiral Howard, who himself had previously been implicated in colluding with pirates, the lord admiral sent his secretary, Humphrey Jobson, to investigate. Hawkins argued that he had never acted unlawfully and that these allegations were part of a conspiracy by his enemies to have him removed from his position. Over the course of the next few years, Hawkins would be fined multiple times, removed from his office, and even briefly thrown into prison.

He hadn't realized it, but much had changed in Plymouth while he had been imprisoned in Spain. Outsiders with crown support, like Sir Ferdinando Gorges, were loosening the grip that local gentry had on the city. Gorges, who had been sent to redevelop Plymouth Fort, observed that piracy in the West Country was directly tied to higher rates of unemployment resulting from peacetime. He believed that he could eradicate the scourge by establishing Plymouth Port as vital to national defense and employing pirates and former privateers in colonization. Gorges was able to persuade many among the West Country gentry to take the profits they had previously earned from pirating and invest in imperial expansion.[35] Recognizing that Londoners were centering their efforts on developing the Virginia colony, Gorges encouraged the West Country gentry to colonize the region that would become New England because of its promising fisheries.

Although piracy seemed to be less attractive to the mariners of the West Country, foreign observers like Spanish ambassador Don Pedro de Zúñiga believed that the region's new focus on colonization was just "the most useful way they have found to play the pirate."[36] And these "colonizing pirates" found a welcome home in New England.

PIRATES AND RELIGION

Although most of those who came to New England in the early seventeenth century did so out of concern for the security of their immortal souls, there were those who ventured across the Atlantic in search of economic freedom and upward social mobility. In many ways, the two were not mutually exclusive. According to historian Mark Hanna, one of the elements of the Protestant Reformation's narrative was that, although "support of private sea marauding against the Spanish...might be piracy according to man's laws," it was entirely aligned with Puritan principles. James I, a staunch Calvinist, already felt personally aggrieved by the "hawkish Puritans" who threatened to upend his pursuit of civil peace. King James I, hoping to rid himself of this possibility, used the Puritans' sanction of commerce raiding as justification for pushing both pirates and Puritans westward.[37] So, many of those who left England brought their West Country and Puritan traditions along with them, including the proclivity for straddling the line between piracy and privateering, legal commerce and illicit trade. John Smith noted in his autobiography that "in all Seas much frequented, there are some Pirates" and found it "incredible how many great and rich Prizes the little Barques of the West Country daily brought home" despite the "bad Life, Qualities and Conditions of Pirates."[38] But there was one unintended consequence of English pirates spreading to the colonies. The Privy Council feared that pirates' proliferation abroad was an indication that the king was incapable of enforcing his sovereignty over peripheral communities. One need only look to Sir Robert Rich, Second Earl of Warwick, to see that the Privy Council was right to be worried.

Sir Robert Rich, often referred to simply as Warwick, epitomized the intimate connection between piracy, colonization, and intense religious devotion. Warwick, born to a noble family, was raised as a devout Puritan. His father maintained a fleet of ships, which he used to conduct "private wars." When Warwick inherited his father's fleet, he furthered his father's legacy and used the fleet to help support his numerous colonial investments. In the early years of English colonization, most colonial ventures were undertaken by private investors with the permission or a charter from the crown. Men like Warwick found plundering to be integral to successful colonization. Although James I made repeated public efforts to deal with the scourge, foreign ambassadors accused the English crown of continuing its support of piracy. Don Zúñiga once again criticized the English king, arguing that the only apparent purpose for these private investors to establish English colonies was "that it appears to them good for pirates."[39] He wasn't wrong. Warwick, who was either invested in or politically involved in no fewer than five colonizing companies, used the financial gains from the ventures of his "private men-of-war," often referred to as "Warwick's men." And Warwick was indispensable in the development of New England. He used his political clout and financial means to help emigrating Puritans obtain charters to establish the colonies of New Plymouth, Rhode Island, Massachusetts Bay, and Connecticut. The town of Warwick, Rhode Island, was named in gratitude for his patronage. As Warwick's fleet ferried immigrants and supplies to the colonies and provided them with maritime defense, the colonists in turn "fitted out, victualed, and fenced the booty" that Warwick's men brought in.[40] As most of them were Puritans themselves, they saw their activities as service to God. In a letter directed to Sir Thomas Smyth, Warwick's peer and the father-in-law of his youngest sister, the author relished in the "robbinge of the Spanyards (as being lyms of Antechrist)" and commended the perpetrators for their service.[41]

KING JAMES AND UNREST

During the reign of James I, many of these pious plunderers were careful to either conceal their activities or misdirect the ire of authorities. Try as he might, James I did not statistically live up to his reputation as a pirate hunter. And some scholars believe that within the first fifteen years of his reign, there were ten times the number of pirates that had existed during Queen Elizabeth I's entire reign.[42] As James I grew increasingly ill in the early 1620s—suffering from gout, severe arthritis, and problems with his liver—he began to lose his grip over the kingdom, especially Parliament. The political sharks were quickly circling, hoping to garner influence over the king's heir apparent, Charles. Despite his ill health, King James

I attempted to secure future peace with Spain by negotiating a marriage between his son and the daughter of King Philip III, Maria Anna. Not only did the move prove incredibly unpopular among the English public and James I's court, but negotiations also ended in humiliating failure, setting into motion a growing rift between the crown and Parliament. When Parliament pressured King James I to declare war against Spain in 1624, voting to release £300,000 to conduct naval attacks, the king refused. But in early March 1625, James I came down with a serious case of malaria and subsequently had a stroke. Physically weakened, the king died on March 27 after being unable to overcome a brutal assault on his body from dysentery.

All of the king's efforts to foster a pacifist approach to rule were for naught. Not one year after his death, war broke out between the English and the Spanish. Within a decade of assuming his position as king, Charles I also faced growing civil unrest and rebellion against his authority. In a series of interconnected religious and political conflicts between 1639 and 1653, collectively referred to as the Wars of the Three Kingdoms, support from England's colonies was divided. Generally, older colonies like Virginia and Maryland supported the crown (Royalists) while newer colonies, like Massachusetts Bay, supported Parliament (Parliamentarians). The final of these conflicts, the English Civil War (1642–51), had a significant impact on England's overseas possessions.[43] After King Charles I was executed for alleged treason in 1649, Royalist colonies immediately recognized his son, King Charles II, as the rightful ruler of the kingdom. Considering those colonies to be in rebellion and hoping to undermine the Royalist war effort, Parliament passed An Act for Prohibiting Trade with the Barbadoes, Virginia, Bermuda and Antego in October 1650. The act labeled the inhabitants of those colonies "notorious Robbers and Traitors" who were, by virtue of English law, barred from conducting any "maner of Commerce or Traffique with any people whatsoever." Further, the act authorized any ship employed by Parliament or any private men-of-war "to seize, surprize and take" any and all vessels and goods belonging to anyone, of any nation, caught "Trading or going to Trade, or coming from Trading with the said Rebels."[44] Parliament's purpose may have been to weaken their opposition. But everyone knows that encouraging bad behavior begets more bad behavior until you lose control of the situation entirely.

PART II

THE BUCCANEERS TAKE THE SEA (CIRCA 1650–1689)

Chapter 3
IMPERIAL GROWING PAINS

It's like the more money we come across, the more problems we see.
—Notorious B.I.G.

As England managed its internal struggle, many of the English colonies in North America were thriving. New Englanders developed an impressive shipbuilding industry, which enabled New England's merchants to create a steady income by consistently exporting the region's natural resources. The colonies enjoyed a period of relative self-governance due to the English government's laissez-faire attitude, which allowed them to handle sea marauding however they saw fit. Even though they sometimes had to protect their maritime commerce from themselves, for much of the seventeenth century, New Englanders didn't really consider piracy a capital crime—a marked departure from traditional English maritime law.[45] Even when their own inhabitants turned pirate and attacked vessels in New England waters, vexed colonists still tended to treat pirates more as a common irritant than a scourge of the seas. The first recorded pirate attacks in New England waters, committed by Dixie Bull and his crew, offer a prime example.[46] Little is known of Bull's early life. Scholars believe that in 1627, Bull apprenticed as a skinner to his older brother Seth, who specialized in the skin and fur trades. Although it is unclear why, Bull did not finish his apprenticeship and left London in 1631. He stayed in Boston for a short time before settling on the coast of Maine thanks to a land grant from Sir Ferdinando Gorges.[47] Hoping to strike it rich trading in beaver furs with the local Indigenous populations, Bull became a familiar face from Maine to New Hampshire.

MESS WITH THE BULL, GET THE HORNS

By all accounts, Dixie Bull did not appear to be on a path toward becoming a pirate. But when life deals you a bad hand, sometimes you find yourself abandoning your principles to seek revenge. In June 1632, Bull was traveling along the Penobscot River, stopping frequently to trade, when he was attacked by a crew of French pirates. Not only did the pirates steal his entire cargo, including "coats, ruggs, blanketts, [and] bisketts," but they took his shallop, too, leaving him all but destitute.[48] Bull first turned to the local government for help in getting financially compensated for his losses and bringing the French to justice. But he quickly realized that the only way he was going to get restitution was by taking the matter into his own hands. After managing to obtain a new vessel, Bull recruited fifteen local Englishmen by proposing a straightforward mission: destroy the French and get rich in the process. This crew, built on a foundation of revenge, spent the waning summer months sailing the New England coast in search of the French. But it seemed that the French had gone stealth, evading the watchful eyes of Bull and his men. Before long, the men realized that their supplies were nearly spent, leaving them with two options: return home empty-handed or plunder any ship, even if it was an English ship.

The crew chose the latter, and they wasted no time seizing several small vessels belonging to local English traders and pressing some of their sailors into piracy. They were now, in the eyes of the law, pirates. Their next target was the trading post at Pemaquid Harbor.[49] Facing little resistance, the pirates pillaged the settlement and the ships anchored in the harbor, stealing goods worth upward of £500—the equivalent of over $135,000 today.[50] The venture did, however, cost them Bull's second-in-command, who was shot and killed as the pirates weighed anchor to depart. Captain Walter Neal, governor of New Hampshire, sent an urgent letter to the governor of Massachusetts Bay, John Winthrop, informing him about Bull's recent piratical exploits and warning him that the pirates could strike again at any time.[51] In his capacity as the military officer of the Piscataqua militia, Captain Neal also requested assistance from Governor Winthrop to put an end to Bull's terror. In the meantime, Bull's crew was

The Sinking Pinnace, illustration by C.J. Staniland and J.R. Wells, 1884. *Courtesy of the Hathi-Trust.*

badly shaken by the loss of one of their own. So, when the pirates seized a ship captained by Anthony Dicks of Salem, the crew demanded that Bull convince Captain Dicks to help them escape to Virginia, which had a reputation for being a hospitable place for pirates. Unfortunately, Bull wasn't quite as menacing as he probably needed to be. Captain Dicks refused to take them to Virginia, so the pirates released him to his ship and turned their attention back to attacking New England's maritime commerce.[52]

Toward the end of 1632, Governor Winthrop dispatched John Gallup, a distinguished sea captain, and a force of about twenty men to join Captain Neal's expedition against the pirates.[53] In all, there were three shallops and two pinnaces with a complement of some sixty men ready to hunt Bull and his crew. But they were immediately delayed for three weeks due to a storm. By the time the pirate hunters set sail, the pirates had taken advantage of their head start and escaped. After two long and wasted months, Captain Neal called off the mission and ordered the ships back home. What happened to Bull after this episode is a mystery. According to Governor Winthrop, the pirates allegedly sent a letter "directed to all the governors, signifying their intent not to do harm to any more of their countrymen, but to go to the southward" and advised the governors "not to send against them; for they were resolved to sink themselves rather than be taken."[54] Winthrop was told that, in February 1633, three of Bull's men, "filled with such Fear and Horrour, that they were afraid of the very Rattling of the Ropes," deserted the pirates and returned home. When questioned about Bull's whereabouts, they said that he had gone with the French.[55] Others, like Captain Roger Clap, believed that Bull met a grisly fate. According to Clap, he was informed directly by one of Bull's former prisoners, Captain Dicks, that Bull had made his way to England when "God destroyed this wretched Man."[56]

The (Alleged) Adulterous Cannibal Pirate

Divine providence may have saved New England traders from the "wicked Device[s]" of Bull and his crew, but they were soon faced with the depraved actions of Captain John Stone, who was once accused of committing cannibalism.[57] Stone was described as a man "who carried himself very proudly, and spake contemptuously of our Magistrates, and carried it lewdly in his Conversation." And that was the least of his misdeeds. He had been pirating in the West Indies for some time before coming to Plymouth. Stone arrived in a small vessel carrying some salt and cows. But news preceded him accusing Stone of seizing the pinnace of a Plymouth councilman. Although it is said that Stone had been drinking heavily and had released the vessel without taking anything, the governor, Edward Winslow, sent Captain Myles Standish to arrest him on suspicion of piracy. It would not be the first time Stone was arrested on charges of piracy. But when Winthrop tried to send Stone to England in order to face charges in an admiralty court, Plymouth residents feared reproach and a marred reputation. Knowing that "it could be no piracy" without their concurrence, Stone was ultimately released.[58] But Stone was unrepentant. Winthrop recounted in his journal how Stone continued to drink excessively and cause trouble. One night while in Boston, Stone was "found upon the bed" with another man's wife and was taken before Winthrop, who determined that Stone should remain in town to await trial. Winthrop ordered that Stone's pinnace should be stayed to prevent him from escaping. Angered, Stone went to the magistrate, Roger Ludlow, "and used braving and threatening speeches against him," allegedly calling the justice a "just ass." Stone was quickly arrested, and the governor "put him in irons, and kept a guard upon him till the court." Ultimately, the "great jury" found insufficient evidence to prosecute Stone for adultery, but they ordered him to pay a £100 fine and he was banished from the Massachusetts Bay Colony "upon pain of death."[59]

But if the residents of Plymouth and Massachusetts Bay thought they were free of the pirate Captain Stone, they couldn't have been more wrong. During the summer of 1633, Stone left Boston and headed to the settlement of Acomenticus in Maine, where he met with Captain Walter Norton.[60] From there, the men and a small crew headed to Virginia, stopping at the mouth of the Connecticut River to allegedly trade with the local Indigenous peoples along the way. Just prior to Stone's arrival, a political quarrel between Dutchmen from their trading post at present-day Hartford and the local Pequot had turned violent. Seeking redress for a violation of the treaty between the two groups, the Dutch pretended to trade with the grand sachem, Tatobem. But when Tatobem boarded their boat, the Dutch held the grand sachem hostage, demanding a bushel of wampum for his release.[61] According to the Pequot, they immediately paid the ransom for Tatobem's return. The Dutch did, indeed, send Tatobem back to shore. But not before ending his life, which "much exasperated our [the Pequot's] spirits, and made us vow a revenge."[62] So, when "suddenly after came these Captaines with a vessell into the River, and pretended to trade with us as the former did," the Pequot exacted their retribution.

The events that followed served as a catalyst for the outbreak of the Pequot War (1636–38), New England's first sustained conflict with the region's Indigenous peoples. Initial reports stated that when Stone and his men entered the mouth of the Connecticut River, three of the men went to shore to kill fowl but were "cut off" by a group of Pequot. Then, the deceased sachem's son, Sassacus, along with some of his men, boarded Stone's vessel. According to John Underhill, captain of the Massachusetts Bay Colony militia, Sassacus entered Captain Stone's cabin and ordered his men to "proceed against the rest [of the English]." Meanwhile, "Captaine Stone having drunke more then did him good, fell backwards on the bed asleepe," affording Sassacus the opportunity to take a small hatchet that he had concealed upon his person and strike Stone on the head. Stone's men, "spying trecherie," made for the cook's room to seek shelter. Some accounts say that a brief tussle between the two groups led to the ship's powder kegs being accidentally ignited, causing the ship to explode. Underhill's account claims that a Pequot ambassador informed him that Stone's men purposely set fire to the powder in order to kill the Pequot. But the Pequot, whom Underhill referred to as "these devils instruments," saw the fire and jumped overboard to save themselves, leaving the English on board to be "blowne up."[63]

Others say that while at the mouth of the river, Stone abducted several Western Niantic women and children to sell into slavery in Virginia.[64] Later testimony from a Pequot messenger related that when Captain Stone first entered the Connecticut River, he had also kidnapped two Pequot men, bound their hands, and forced them to help pilot the crew up the river, which they did. At that point, three of Stone's men went to shore with their Pequot captives and made camp for the night. Unbeknownst to them, a small rescue party had followed Stone and his men upriver. Under the cover of darkness, the Pequot attacked and killed the sleeping captors, freeing the prisoners. According to the messenger's account, the Pequot then approached Stone's pinnace, but it "suddenly blew up into the air" before they could take it.[65] Captain Roger Clap certainly believed Stone to be guilty of malice against the Pequot. When he learned that some of the Pequot reported that they had "roasted him [Stone] alive," Clap rejoiced that "thus did God destroy him that so proudly threatned to ruin us by complaining against us."[66] And this is how an alleged adulterous cannibal pirate named Captain Stone helped kickstart a brutal and bloody war in colonial New England.

WAR AND PROFIT

Aside from the exploits of Dixie Bull and Captain Stone, records about piracy in New England before 1642 are scant, most likely due to the region's engagement in the Pequot War. But with the outbreak of the English Civil War, many in the colonies saw new opportunities to profit from commerce raiding. The colonies, especially in New England, directly benefited from the exploits of privateers acting on behalf of Parliament and its supporters. And they were about to experience the gifts of providence in more ways than one. Before the war, the previously mentioned pious plunderer, Robert Rich, Second Earl of Warwick, became one of the founding members of the Providence Island Company, chartered in 1631. The company's primary purpose was to establish an ideal Puritan commonwealth on the "newly discovered" island off the east coast of Nicaragua.[67] But it didn't hurt that the island was ideally located for harassing the Spanish Main.

One of the company's commissioned privateers was Captain William Jackson, who spent the late 1630s in the West Indies taking Spanish ships as prizes to support the Providence Island Colony. In late August 1639, during one of his stops to refit and refuel, Jackson landed on the coast of

Massachusetts Bay Colony, much to the delight of the colonists. Governor Winthrop recorded in his journal that Jackson brought with him "much wealth in money, plate, indico [indigo], and sugar." After selling his stock of indigo and sugar for £1,400, Jackson then used some of the hard Spanish currency he'd previously pilfered to furnish "himself with commodities, and departed again for the West Indies."[68] The influx of hard specie was most welcome for colonists, who suffered during frequent currency crises.[69] Plunder, particularly in the form of currency, was a saving grace for the colonies. And colonists didn't seem to care whether it came from pirates or privateers. Winthrop noted that by 1640, "scarcity of money made a great change in all commerce," as English merchants would only accept hard currency as payment for goods and services. At the same time, the prices of land and cattle fell by half, then one-third, before bottoming out at one-quarter, leaving many in New England in financial ruin, unable to "pay their debts though they had enough."[70] They worried whether they could survive this latest monetary predicament. But with civil war in England on the horizon, New Englanders were about to witness how "combining faithful settlement with aggressive plunder" could reveal God's divine providence.[71]

Eleven years after King Charles I had dissolved Parliament and ruled England without them, he found himself on the verge of bankruptcy. The expense of conflicts like the Bishops' Wars and civil unrest drained the already sparse royal coffers, and the king had limited options when it came to increasing the treasury's revenue. His financial distress came to a head toward the end of 1640 during the Second Bishops' War. Charles I found himself in a mortifying position: no one was willing to grant him a loan or offer financial support for further military campaigns against the Scottish Covenanters. Without any viable options, the king begrudgingly signed a preliminary agreement called the Treaty of Ripon. The agreement essentially said that the Scots would continue to occupy the English counties of Durham and Northumberland and be paid £850 per day until an acceptable final settlement could be reached. The English were also responsible for reimbursing the Scots for their wartime expenses. Not only was King Charles I humiliated by the treaty's demands, but he had no choice but to recall Parliament. He could not hope to raise the funds necessary to fulfill the financial terms of the treaty without Parliament, which had the sole authority to raise taxes.

But Charles I's reunion with Parliament was far from amicable, and Parliament made their authority quite clear to the king. Between coercing Charles I to assent to the beheading of his right-hand man for

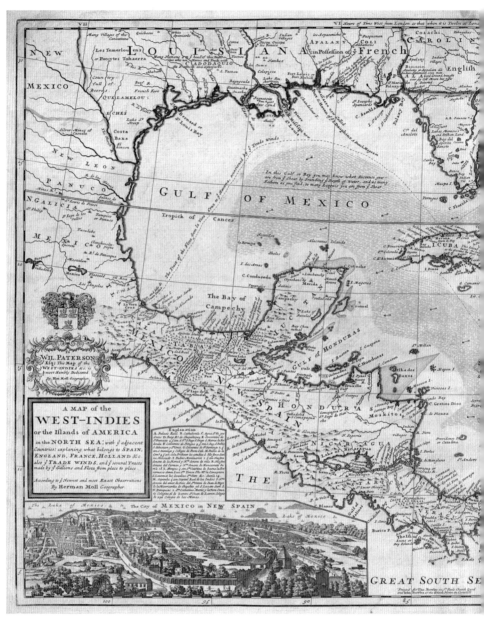

A Map of the West-Indies or the Islands of America in the North Sea, by Herman Moll, circa 1720. Courtesy of Geographicus Rare Antique Maps.

"treason" and forcing his assent to an act that forbade the dissolution of the English Parliament without their consent, Parliament used the king to effectively whittle away his own power. Charles I tried to reassert his royal authority as tensions mounted by removing Algernon Percy, Tenth Earl of Northumberland, from his position as lord high admiral in June 1642 for openly defying royal authority. Northumberland was the highest-ranking member of King Charles I's court to ally with the Parliamentarians. When Northumberland, "a Person of known Integrity and Honour," was dismissed, Parliament appointed the Earl of Warwick admiral of the fleet, giving him the "Power to grant Commissions, and to remove or displace all Officers, and other Persons whatsoever" under his command.[72] Appointing Warwick, who was an outspoken Puritan leader and vocal critic of King Charles I during his "personal rule," was Parliament's line in the sand. And just two months later, the First English Civil War began.

Warwick wasted no time in using his new position as Parliament's lord high admiral to wreak havoc on the Spanish and launder plunder through colonial ports. This earned him the nickname "Warwick the Public *Pyrat*" from Royalists. Warwick, who had been impressed by Captain Jackson's earlier ventures, personally commissioned Jackson in late 1642 to amass a small fleet. One of the captains who joined Jackson's fleet was Thomas Cromwell, a noted seaman from Massachusetts Bay. They cruised the West Indies for several months raiding towns throughout the Spanish Main, such as Maracaibo and Trujillo.[73] In 1643, Jackson and Cromwell sacked Saint Jago de la Vega, capital of Jamaica under Spanish rule. The privateers—pirates in the eyes of the Spanish—held the city hostage until the Spanish government agreed to provide them with provisions, commodities, and 7,000 pieces of eight. They continued to plunder over the next few years, returning to New England several times and even bringing enslaved Africans and Indigenous people to Boston.[74] In his journal, William Bradford, governor of Plymouth Colony, described the "warr-like" arrival of three privateers in the middle of May 1646, one of which was commanded by Cromwell. With a commission from the Earl of Warwick, Cromwell and his fellow privateers "had taken sundrie prizes" from Spaniards in the West Indies. In Winthrop's account, he described how Captain Cromwell had "taken four or five Spanish vessels," which had been filled with "great riches." According to Bradford, there were approximately eighty "lustie men" on board who were most unruly.[75] He described their behavior on shore as being no better, becoming like "madd-men" after they "did so distemper them selves with drinke." Fortunately, the men—who spent lavishly—became "more moderate & orderly" in the weeks they stayed in Plymouth. Winthrop praised the privateers, who "spent liberally and gave freely to many of the poorer sort [in Plymouth]."[76]

In June 1646, Cromwell and the other privateers headed to Massachusetts Bay Colony, during which time they again "spente and scattered a great deale of money." Winthrop noted that Cromwell and his crew had "much

A pirate ship attacking a merchant's ship, artist unknown, 2005. An adaptation of Ambroise Louise Garneray's 1852 painting *La Prise du Kent par Surcouf*. *Wikimedia Commons.*

money, and great store of plate and jewels of great value," which they had little trouble spending among Boston's merchants. Cromwell also gave Governor Winthrop a "very fair" sedan chair he had seized, which the captain said was meant to be a gift from Don Garcia Sarmiento Sotomayor, the viceroy of Mexico, to his sister in Spain.[77] Bradford, however, was much more cautious of the commissioned rogues than Winthrop. While Bradford believed Cromwell and his men brought more sin than money, Winthrop felt the colonists should be grateful for the "divine providence" that brought the marauders' to Plymouth. Clearly, God saw fit to use the brigands "for the comfort and help of that town, which was now almost deserted," sending a "strong north west wind" to force Cromwell and his crew into Plymouth Harbor.[78] Winthrop even went so far as to paint Cromwell in a divine light. He noted that Cromwell, who had been offered boarding at the finest places in town, chose instead to stay in a "poor thatched house." When asked why he refused better lodging, Cromwell replied that the poor man who owned this "mean estate…entertained him, when others would not, and therefore he would not leave him now, when he might do him good."[79]

Winthrop's depiction of Cromwell as a charitable and humble man ignores, whether intentional or misguided, Cromwell's lengthy history of maritime violence and depredations. Certainly, Cromwell socially benefited from having the endorsement of such a pious and important man, even if that endorsement had been bought. But Winthrop and the New England colonies were financially rewarded by supporting men like Cromwell. It was especially advantageous for New Englanders when these privateers were backed by the Earl of Warwick, who had been a crucial figure in the region's successful political and economic development. But they had to be careful not to run afoul of said benefactors. After Cromwell left Boston, "well maned & victuled," to voyage into the West Indies again, Warwick learned of Cromwell's extravagant spending and gift-giving in New England.[80] Incensed, Warwick believed Cromwell conspired with New England merchants to deny him his rightful share of the prizes. In December 1646, he sent a letter to Boston merchants Adam Winthrop, David Yale, Anthony Stoddard, and Benjamin Gilliam requesting that they assist him or face legal action. Warwick informed the Boston merchants that he would be sending William Penoyre, a merchant from London, to retrieve the "goods of great value belonging to him [Warwick], detained by Captain Cromwell." Penoyre was authorized to receive these goods because they had been "taken by virtue of Captain Jackson's commission" and therefore were not Cromwell's to sell or give away. Fortunately for the New England economy, the merchants of Boston must have made things right with Warwick. Three years after leaving New England, Cromwell, having taken "sundry prizes," returned to Massachusetts Bay a rich man without further complaint from Warwick.[81]

Chapter 4
THE PROTECTORATE,
THE RESTORATION, AND THE GLORIOUS REVOLUTION

The monarchy is part of the state. It exists to serve the people.
—Heather Brooke[82]

If the colonists thought politics had been messy during the English Civil War, things were about to get much more complicated. After the execution of King Charles I in 1649, the Rump Parliament adopted An Act Declaring England to Be a Commonwealth, which was a political structure governing England, Ireland, Scotland, and Wales as a republic. Although the war continued until 1651, the Rump Parliament was supposed to be in the process of developing a working constitution, after which they would dissolve themselves. But in April 1653, Oliver Cromwell, hero of the English Civil War, learned that Parliament had not only failed to deliver a constitution, they were trying to remain in session despite their promise of dissolution. Backed by the Army Council, Cromwell used military force to physically eject members of Parliament from the chamber, ending the session. And on December 16, 1653, Cromwell was appointed lord protector, a position he held until his death in 1658.

What Cannot Defend Itself
Shall Not Be Defended

While the crown and Parliament had been locked in battle against each other, many New England merchants and mariners had turned to their colonial governors to legitimize their sea marauding. These governors issued their own letters of marque, which authorized the holder to seize the merchant vessels of enemies and to blockade enemy ports in the West Indies. Colonial governors justified the issuance of these letters as being in line with their duty to protect their colonies against French and Dutch pirates.[83] Sometimes it's better to ask for forgiveness than for permission. With the English government distracted, New England increased its trade with the West Indies, knowing that this was "where the buccaneers or pirates at this time were numerous."[84] Trading with pirates and privateers who operated in the West Indies brought significant amounts of bullion into the New England economy, which they desperately needed.[85] So much bullion was arriving that it necessitated the creation of a mint to prevent fraud (even though this was prohibited). According to Hanna, New England's production of coinage, which they called pine tree shillings, was "both a real and symbolic illustration of New England's overt support of illicit sea marauding." This was perhaps best exemplified in the Hull family of Massachusetts Bay.

While working as a silversmith in Boston, John Hull had earned a good reputation for his skills. In May 1652, the Massachusetts General Court decided to establish their own (technically illegal) mint in Boston and appointed John Hull as mint master. To cover the costs of melting, refining, and coining, Hull was allowed to keep for himself fifteen pence out of every twenty shillings. The arrangement enabled him to amass a considerable fortune, which he often invested in private men-of-war. Meanwhile, John's younger brother, Edward Hull, sought his fortune at sea. Edward received a commission from the Rhode Island Assembly to seize Dutch vessels around the summer of 1652, although he soon preyed on French ships as well. Rhode Island assumed it had admiralty jurisdiction, which authorized the assembly to commission privateers, who served as a critical line of defense for the vulnerable colony. There was one small problem for Edward in that he received his commission about a month *after* he'd captured a prize. He was clearly educated in the art of seeking forgiveness, not permission. Additionally, the Dutch considered the commission invalid because it did not come from the English crown, making Edward a pirate.[86]

A depiction of the pirate Captain George Lowther and his company at Port Mayo in the Gulph of Matique, engraving from *History of Most Famous Highway Men* by Captain Charles Johnson, 1734. *Courtesy of the Library of Congress.*

One of Edward's victims, Captain Kempo Seibada, decided to bring a suit against the entire Hull family in November 1652. According to the court records, Seibada sued Robert (the family patriarch) and John as "part owners and setters-forth" of the *Swallow* "under the command of Edward Hull, pirate, for damages of his estate in taking out his house at Block Island by said Edward Hull, goods to the value of £96." Further, Seibada alleged that the defendants "had been receivers of part of the booties that Edward Hull took" and that father and brother were guilty of concealing Edward's estate. Despite numerous testimonies against them, Robert and John were able to show the court some letters they had sent to Edward condemning his actions and that they "did endeavor to improve all the interest wee had in him to gaine him from that imploym[ent]." Ultimately, Robert and John were acquitted of the charges against them. And Edward? He failed to appear at his trial, escaping to London. So, we'll never know what Edward's fate would have been.[87]

THE PIRATES FIND A REFUGE

Although the 1650s and 1660s marked the rise of the buccaneering phase of the golden age of piracy, there were astonishingly few pirate attacks along the North American coast. During Cromwell's rule over the Commonwealth, he envisioned strengthening the empire and establishing commercial supremacy over competing empires through the three Ps: "piety, plunder, and plantation."[88] During the Anglo-Spanish War (1654–60), he developed a plan known as the Western Design, which was modeled on the Providence Island Company's scheme from the 1630s. Cromwell would destroy Spain's power in the West Indies by establishing a permanent English base in the Caribbean, which would enable English privateers to more easily disrupt the shipping lanes between Europe and the Spanish Main. If they could wipe out the Spanish, England could finally have a reliable source of bullion.[89]

To garner support for the Western Design, Cromwell made sure that it was couched in religious justifications. According to a manifesto by Cromwell's secretary, John Milton, Spain was not in the West Indies planting colonies in uninhabited locales but, rather, stealing land from Indigenous communities. Milton used the Black Legend as defense of England's interference, arguing that the English were truly the "Avengers of the Murder of that People, and of the Injuries sustain'd by them."[90] Many of New England's clergymen and devout colonial leaders supported the Commonwealth's design. They did not see plundering the Spanish as incongruous with their faith. For example, Reverend John Cotton of Massachusetts Bay predicted the Western Design would initiate events that would lead to the drying up of the Euphrates River, culminating in Armageddon and the second coming of Jesus. Rhode Island's governor, Roger Williams, agreed with Cotton, believing that if the Protestants did not act quickly and aggressively to seize the treasure of the West Indies, it would be used by the Spanish to further fuel the "Popish Leviathan."[91]

Based on the advice of Thomas Gage, a former Catholic missionary who had spent many years ministering to imprisoned English pirates, their best option for a base was either Hispaniola or Cuba.[92] Gage, incorrectly, believed that these islands were poorly defended and therefore could be easily taken. They first targeted Hispaniola, but the Spanish were able to swiftly repulse the untrained English troops who suffered heavy losses—mostly from disease. After their failure at Hispaniola, the English turned their attention to Jamaica, which turned out to *actually* be weakly defended. The English successfully seized the island from the Spanish in the summer of 1655, and it soon became a haven for pirates. Within a few years, all the powerful naval vessels and most of the soldiers that had conquered Jamaica left when their dreams of instant wealth were dashed, and they were faced with the prospect of a grisly death at the hands of any number of tropical diseases. Leaving the island essentially defenseless, the colonial governors who ran the colony turned to the buccaneers, offering them letters of marque in exchange for securing the Jamaican coastline.[93]

From Port Royal to Boston: A Heavenly Match

Although Cromwell's son, Richard, succeeded as lord protector, he was dismissed less than a year later. After much backdoor political maneuvering, Charles, Prince of Wales, returned to England. He was crowned King Charles II in the Restoration of the Monarchy in 1660. Commerce raiders once again wondered what their status would be under new leadership: pirate or privateer? National hero or villain? The waves of political and religious turmoil between the 1660s and 1680s would offer no easy answer. Shortly after King Charles II's coronation, the newly assembled Parliament wasted no time in trying to assert Anglican dominance. Between 1661 and 1665, Parliament passed a series of acts, which collectively came to be known as the Clarendon Code. They included the Corporation Act of 1661, which required any municipal officeholder to swear allegiance to the Church of England, and the Act of Uniformity of 1662, which made the use of the Anglican Book of Common Prayer compulsory. Meanwhile, King Charles II's conduct over the first decade of his reign slowly eroded his congenial relationship with Parliament.

During the transition between the protectorate and the monarchy's restoration, the pirates and privateers who came to Jamaica quickly established an unofficial home on the southeast side of the island. They settled at the end of an eighteen-mile-long tombolo, or sand spit, at Point Cagway, a small town sitting on approximately fifty acres of land at the mouth of Kingston Harbor. We know it today as Port Royal. And by 1670, it had come to be referred to as the "wickedest city on earth." At that time, there were fewer than 8,000 white inhabitants living in Jamaica. But there were an estimated 1,500 pirates and privateers based in Port Royal alone.[94] The establishment of Jamaica as a base for attacking Spanish shipping coincided with a dramatic increase in pirates and so-called privateers throughout the

Marooned, by Howard Pyle, 1887. *Wikimedia Commons*.

1670s and 1680s. So, where did all these pirates go when they weren't in Jamaica? Sir James Modyford, a chief judge of Jamaica's court of admiralty, pointed to New England. Describing the return of Henry Morgan and his privateers after they pillaged Portobelo, Modyford explains that with their "plunder in jewells, gold and silver," some of the privateers headed to "Old [England]," while "more [made] for New England." And the New England colonies were more than eager to provide the pirates with an open market for their loot.[95]

One of the reasons New England colonies seemed more receptive to trading with pirates is that they were primarily charter (or private) colonies. This meant that unlike royal colonies, whose governors were directly appointed by the crown and bound by instructions from the Privy Council, their governors were typically elected from among the freemen of the colony. As residents of the colony, many of those who got elected governor were generally already allied with the colony's merchants before running for office. Those outside New England often complained that, because the governor is elected annually by their peers, they "endeavour to do nothing that may disoblige their Electors, lest the next year they are deprived of their Dignities." Local merchants in the late seventeenth century often had a vested interest in making sure the colony maintained a solid relationship with pirates because it enabled them to amass great fortunes. So, if their governor was of an anti-pirate mindset, the merchants would exert immense pressure on the governor to force their compliance. And it wasn't just the merchants the governors had to worry about. Some colonial governors and council members would "complain they are hardly safe in their Persons or Estates; if by a due and vigorous execution of the Law against Pyrats or illegal Traders, they should incense the People against them."[96]

In a letter to the Lords of Trade and Plantations dated February 28, 1684, Sir Thomas Lynch, governor of Jamaica, highlighted the extent of the relationship between pirates and the New England colonies, particularly noting the economic and political impact it had on New England. According to Lynch, the "colonists are now full of pirates' money," because England's laws against pirates "neither discourage nor lessen them" when they can find refuge in places like New England. And why would the colonists shun the pirates when the colonists' pockets were overflowing with pirate money? Lynch stated that he had received a report out of Boston, a city once referred to as the "common receptacle of pirates of all nations," which claimed that pirates had lately brought £80,000 into the city. One contemporary noted that the colonists "are too much addicted to abet and encourage both Pyrats and illegal Traders."[97]

AN ENGLISHMAN, A DUTCHMAN, AND A *FLYING HORSE*

Parliament became frustrated by King Charles II's handling of foreign policy, which dragged the English into several costly wars. In one of his more egregious political mistakes, Charles II negotiated and signed a treaty with France called the Treaty of Dover in 1670, of which there were two versions: one secret, one public. In the secret version, Charles II, who was in serious financial trouble, agreed that he would profess his conversion to Catholicism "as soon as the affairs of his kingdom permitted" in return for monetary compensation. King Louis XIV agreed to pay Charles II a one-time sum of £200,000 for his conversion and supply six thousand French troops to suppress any opposition or rebellion. Further, Louis XIV agreed to pay Charles II a yearly stipend of nearly £300,000, part of which he was expected to use to provide the French with military assistance against the Dutch. There was one ever so tiny political detail that Charles II conveniently overlooked: England was presently in an alliance with the Dutch.[98]

The secret treaty was signed and sealed on June 1, 1670. To provide cover for his new income and the promise to provide the French with soldiers and men-of-war, King Charles II appointed George Villiers, Second Duke of Buckingham, to negotiate a treaty with King Louis XIV. This public version of the treaty mirrored the secret one but omitted any mention of the religious clauses Charles II had agreed to. Expecting a lengthy back-and-forth, Buckingham was surprised—and a bit suspicious—by the speed and ease with which the treaty came together. This version was then signed by all five of Charles II's high councilors on December 21, 1670. Although no mention of Charles II's promise to convert to Catholicism was expressed, Parliament was also a bit dubious as to the true nature of the treaty.[99]

As France prepared for war against the Dutch early the following year, King Charles II tried to quietly obtain the necessary funding to uphold their end of the new agreement. Although Parliament agreed to allocate money to the Royal Navy under the pretense of protecting English trade, they refused to bankroll a war against a Protestant nation conducted in alliance with a Catholic nation. Parliament was still concerned about Charles II's Catholic leanings. Further, the king found little support among his subjects, especially the merchants whose profit margins were negatively impacted by high French tariffs. Charles II did himself no favors in curbing suspicion about his Catholic sympathies when he issued the Royal Declaration of Indulgence in February 1672. The declaration, which suspended the penal laws that punished recusants from the Church of England, was his response to Parliament's rejection of his financial request. Charles II hoped that, by issuing the declaration, he could gather the support—both political and financial—of the Protestant nonconformists and Catholics in his realms. His efforts were largely unsuccessful.[100]

The Dutch soon became aware of England's betrayal after a naval incident in March 1672 between an English squadron and a Dutch convoy near the Isle of Wight in the English Channel. King Charles II was at the point of no return and officially declared war against the Dutch, kickstarting the Third Anglo-Dutch War (1672–74). The exploits of an Englishman from Boston named John Rhoades, and Captain Jurriaen Aernouts, a Dutch privateer, provide an excellent example of the tangled web woven by such backdoor political maneuvers. In the summer of 1674, Rhoades was a coasting pilot who was presently unemployed when he found himself in New York, once a Dutch colony.[101] The Dutch managed to briefly reclaim the territory during the Third Anglo-Dutch War, returning it to the English at the conclusion of the war. While there, Rhoades met Captain Aernouts of the *Flying Horse*, who was in a most flummoxed state. He was commissioned as a privateer by the governor of Curaçao to "take, plunder, spoil and possess any of the ships, persons, or estates" of any enemy of the Netherlands.[102] When Aernouts received his letter of marque, the Netherlands was embroiled in the Franco-Dutch War (1672–78) and the Third Anglo-Dutch War, which gave Aernouts license to take any French or English ship as legal prize. But when he arrived in New York that summer, he learned that not only was the colony no longer under Dutch control, but the Dutch were no longer at war with the English, having signed the Treaty of Westminster of 1674 nearly six months earlier.[103]

Aernouts was forced to rethink his plans. He decided that, since the Dutch were still at war with the French, he would sail northward toward the French fisheries in the Gulf of St. Lawrence. While Aernouts fitted out the *Flying Horse*, he serendipitously met Rhoades, who told Aernouts that he was very familiar with the coasts of the northern French colonies. Rhoades also noted that he had recently come from Fort Pentagoet and found the defenses of the French colonies in that area were weak.[104] With knowledge of the strength of the French garrison at Pentagoet, Rhoades believed that the fort could be easily taken. Excited by the prospect of conquering the rich fur trade in that area, Aernouts asked his crew if they approved of this course of action, to which they unanimously voted yes. The Dutch privateers needed Rhoades's expertise, and Rhoades needed a job. So, he took the oath of allegiance to the Prince of Orange and became the chief pilot of the *Flying Horse*.[105]

The privateers met with instant success. Reaching Fort Pentagoet on August 1, 1674, they seized the fort after just two hours of fighting and held the fort commander hostage. When Rhoades discovered that the commander was Jacques de Chambly, the governor of Acadia, the privateers demanded payment in the form of one thousand beaver pelts for his release. Unfortunately for de Chambly, he had no way of procuring that many pelts and thus remained hostage as the privateers headed eastward to the Bay of Fundy.[106] In just one month, the privateers were able to take every French fort and trading post along the way, claiming the entire Acadia territory for the Dutch. To secure his claim over the territory, Aernouts placed copies of his privateering commission and statements of legal conquest in bottles, which he buried at each site they captured. Captain Aernouts renamed the area New Holland.[107]

Having filled the *Flying Horse* to the brim with plundered goods, the privateers—most likely at Rhoades's suggestion—sailed to Boston in late September 1674. When they arrived, Captain Aernouts applied to

Who Shall Be Captain, by Howard Pyle, 1911. *Wikimedia Commons.*

Governor John Leverett requesting his consent to sell their spoils and remain in the harbor while they refitted the *Flying Horse*. Governor Leverett gladly granted the request. He authorized the Massachusetts Bay Colony to purchase all of the cannons the privateers had taken out of the French forts. The remainder of the goods were auctioned to the city's merchants. Toward the first of November, the *Flying Horse* was fully refitted, and Captain Aernouts prepared to sail back to Curaçao. Worried that the French might try to reclaim the territory of New Holland, Aernouts decided to put together an expeditionary force and promoted John Rhoades to captain. He also promoted Peter Roderigo and Cornelius Andreson to captain and accepted Bostonian John Williams's enlistment to the force. Before he left, Aernouts authorized Rhoades, Roderigo, Andreson, and Williams to return to New Holland under the flag of Prince William of Orange. While there, the men were expected to foster trade relations with the local Indigenous population and prevent the French from reclaiming the territory until further notice.[108]

While the privateers waited for instructions from the Dutch government, they spent the next several months cruising the waters around New Holland. Most of their time was spent seizing English ships trading with members of the Wabanaki Confederacy, which the English did not have permission from the Dutch to do. One of the men they apprehended for illegally trading in New Holland was Major Nicholas Shapleigh of New Hampshire. While searching Major Shapleigh's vessel, the Dutchmen uncovered a more damning conspiracy. Captain Roderigo found evidence that Shapleigh was ferrying Frenchmen and various provisions from Port Royal, Jamaica, to French settlements along the St. Johns River. Roderigo also suspected that Shapleigh was providing French settlers with ammunition so that they might reclaim some of the lost territory. Although the Dutch ultimately let Shapleigh go, they seized his cargo and confiscated any evidence of his shady dealings with the French.[109]

Before long, news of the Dutch privateer attacks on English ships reached Boston. In February 1675, several complaints had been filed against Captain Rhoades and his Dutch comrades, forcing Governor Leverett to take action. He instructed Captain Samuel Mosely, who had recently been cruising around Nantucket to protect Boston shipping from Dutch attacks, to assemble an armed crew to apprehend the privateers. After a few weeks, Mosely had nearly caught up with them when he crossed paths with a French ship and, launching a surprise attack with the assistance of the French, forced the privateers—who were outmaneuvered and outnumbered—to surrender. They were brought to Boston on April 2, 1675, and imprisoned at Cambridge, Massachusetts, to await trial. Over the next couple of months, each of the men stood trial on charges of piracy. Some of the men confessed to their actions, while others proclaimed their innocence by virtue of their commission. The court held that the commissions were not legal because Captain Aernouts had signed them, not Prince William of Orange. Each of the men was found guilty and sentenced to hang. But not one would find themselves at the end of a noose. A week before the set execution date, King Philip's War (1675–76) broke out in New England. In the chaos, the executions were stayed. Ultimately, the men were pardoned, most of them under the condition that they be banished from the Massachusetts Bay Colony.[110]

The Navigation Acts

While New Englanders were known to pass judgment on the piratical transgressions of the Dutch and French from time to time, they were less inclined to acknowledge their own engagement with piracy. By the 1670s, the New England colonies—especially Massachusetts Bay—had "practically grown into a state of independence under their charter" and bridled at "any encroachments upon the powers of self government." Over the course of his reign, King Charles II tried to increase administrative oversight of the colonies and, with the support of Parliament, issued a series of acts collectively known as the Navigation Acts. The first of these acts was passed upon the restoration of Charles II in 1660. Among the many provisions, the act restricted all colonial imports and exports to English ships. At least three-quarters of the ship's crew had to be English. It also enumerated colonial goods, such as sugar, tobacco, cotton, and wool, which could only be exported to England or other English colonies.[111] Colonial trade was further restricted with the Act of 1663, which required all European goods bound for the colonies to be first trans-shipped through England, where they would be unloaded and inspected. If approved, the goods would be reloaded upon payment of duties. This meant a significant increase in shipping times and cost, which was passed on to the colonists in the form of higher prices. It was also an attempt to force the colonies to rely solely on England for European products, preventing them from forming (or continuing) their own independent trade networks.[112]

The intent may have been to bring the colonists, particularly those in private colonies, under tighter control, but it only increased their resentment. For many New Englanders, the passage of the Navigation Acts took their traditional maritime and trade practices and placed them under the broad umbrella of illicit trade. They were now considered, in the eyes of the crown and their fellow Englishmen across the pond, smugglers and pirates. Undeterred, the colonists of New England continued with business as usual—albeit a bit more cautiously. But by the late 1670s, the New England colonies were firmly on the English government's radar. When agents of the Royal African Company accused the New England colonists of disrupting their trade and harassing their ships, Governor Leverett vehemently denied the allegations. According to Leverett, for over forty years there had not been any piratical attempts "on that navigation by any of our Massachusetts adventurers" and he had no control over "some from England or some Barbadoes merchants that have sent upon that voyage, and taken this way to repair their vessels."[113] But the irregularity of New England trade continued to vex the crown. Lord Vaughn, governor of Jamaica, believed that because "his Majesty receives no Customs for it [irregular trade]," it was "New England men [who] reap the whole profit." He warned the secretary of state, Sir Joseph Williamson, that "unless his Majesty's authority be settled there," New Englanders would ultimately "make the trade of most of the Plantations (as they have their own) independent" from England and encourage greater commerce with pirates. Lord Vaughn suggested that it might be in the king's best interest to take advantage of the "Indians being in rebellion against Plymouth and the Massachusetts." With the New England colonies in a vulnerable position, "his authority might be easily established."[114]

During a meeting of the Lords of Trade and Plantations in February 1676, members decided it was necessary to consider the various points that had been raised regarding the vital importance of making the New England colonies more dependent on the sea crown and reducing the appeal of piracy there. For example, some had suggested that doing so would end the "irregularity of their trade." Others proposed that it would "bring them to such an acknowledgment of his Majesty's authority as to submit" and recognize that they couldn't understand the "superior points" of imperial trade.[115] To determine the best course of action, the crown decided to take advantage of a territorial dispute in New England to conduct reconnaissance on the state of affairs in the colonies. Edward Randolph was dispatched to Boston in March 1676 to deliver a royal letter to the governor and magistrates regarding the dispute.[116] Over the next six months, Randolph prepared a lengthy report organized into twelve observations (mostly focused on Massachusetts Bay), which covered everything from a detailed outline of the legislative and court structures to religious affairs. Of particular concern to the crown with respect to trade and piracy were Randolph's notes on any New England laws that were contrary to England, their general trade practices, their handling of duties and customs fees, and how "generally affected" the colonists were toward the English government.[117]

According to Randolph, the local magistrates "do not mind the letter of the law where their public interest is concerned," but they cared more about the "quality and disposition of the persons than the nature of the offence." And New Englanders viewed any attempt to enforce the laws of England as a "breach of their privileges." As far as their trade practices, Randolph noted that the New England colonies "trade with most parts of Europe from which they directly import all kinds of merchandise," and the inhabitants take "no notice...of the Navigation or Plantation Acts." He also observed that in Boston, duties were collected on imported wine and provisions, taxes were levied on the sale of wine and beer, and they only collected customs

A depiction of the pirate Captain Bartholomew "Black Bart" Roberts with his ships the *Royal Fortune* and the *Ranger* on the coast of Guinea, engraving by Benjamin Cole, circa 1724. *Wikimedia Commons.*

on the exportation of horses. Randolph calculated that Massachusetts Bay Colony's revenue was upward of £20,000, which the governor and magistracy spent on whatever they "think fit without giving any account" to the crown. It seemed obvious why pirates would find themselves welcome in New England with leaders like John Leverett, Thomas Danforth, and Samuel Symonds, who reserved the "power to alter or disannul any law not agreeable with their humour," thereby keeping the region "in slavery."[118]

While in New England, Edward Randolph proved to be a "fit instrument of tyranny," especially against pirates and those who colluded with them. He developed "a most remorseless hatred" toward the Massachusetts Bay Colony's charter and "any who wished to preserve it," becoming one of the primary architects of the charter's demise.[119]

BE WELL TO PORTSMOUTH, AND LET NOT POOR NELLY STARVE

Although King Charles II was preoccupied by the Exclusion Crisis, which threatened his line of succession, and the Rye House Plot, which threatened his life, the king still found time to tighten his control of the New England colonies. Edward Randolph, having completed his observations, brought forth eight charges against Massachusetts Bay Colony that he believed violated their charter and warranted its revocation. Although their obvious collusion with pirates was not explicitly listed, it was implied in two of the charges: maintaining a mint to press their own coins and violating the Navigation Acts, which amounted to an annual loss of £100,000 to the crown's customs.[120] After a formal investigation and a series of court shenanigans, the crown revoked the Massachusetts Bay charter in October 1684. King Charles II, along with the Lords of Trade, then proceeded to plan for the creation of a unified administration to oversee the New England colonies. This new Dominion of New England would have a single governor to help streamline its administration. But just a few months later, in February 1685, King Charles II died. He was succeeded by his brother James, who moved forward with his brother's plan. After a brief period of provisional oversight, Sir Edmund Andros assumed the position of governor of the Dominion of New England in December 1686. As he imposed new taxes, curtailed colonists' rights, and abolished colonial assemblies, Andros became wildly unpopular among New Englanders.

The royal handling of the situation in New England did little to curb the issues of piracy and illicit trade and only enraged the colonists, who were told they had "no more privileges left…than not to be sold as slaves."[121] For example, in 1683, Captain Thomas Paine of Rhode Island went to Jamaica to obtain a privateering commission from the governor, Sir Thomas Lynch, to allegedly seize pirates. But Paine had no such intentions and headed instead to recover silver from a Spanish wreck. Afterward, he joined with several other treasure seekers, including Captain Brehal, who had a commission from the governor of Saint-Domingue, to pillage the Spanish town of St. Augustine. Paine then decided to return to Rhode Island, which would probably not have been noteworthy were it not for the political and legal upheaval in process. Upon learning of Paine's arrival, customs collector William Dyre sent his deputy to investigate. The deputy, satisfied "as to the character of the ship," showed Governor William Coddington his commission and demanded that Coddington assist him in apprehending both Paine and his ship. But Coddington told the deputy that he would assess the situation for himself, and they could reconvene in the morning, "by which time the pirates had time to arm themselves against arrest."[122]

The next morning, Governor Coddington refused to help the deputy seize Paine on account of Paine's commission from Governor Lynch. The deputy asked to see the commission, which Paine offered freely. After inspecting the commission and getting the opinion of others, like Edward Cranfield, governor of New Hampshire, the deputy determined that the commission was a forgery. Everyone but Coddington agreed, citing that "it was not Sir Thomas Lynch's hand, nor were his titles correctly given." Cranfield even described it as "styling him one of the gentlemen of the King's Bedchamber, instead of his Privy Chamber, whereby I knew it to be forged."[123] Although the deputy urged Coddington to arrest Paine, the governor said he would gladly do so *if* the deputy could prove that Paine's commission was false. Coddington also denied the deputy's request for a copy of Paine's commission, making it practically impossible to prove the commission was forged.

Meanwhile, Dyre faced significant obstruction trying to bring a pirate "of the first magnitude, famous in bloodshed and robberies," to justice. He had recently seized a French "privateer," *La Trompeuse*, refitting in Boston. Although he tried to have the Frenchman arrested, his efforts were hampered by several of the local merchants. One of the merchants, Samuel Shrimpton, "supplied, succoured, countenanced and encouraged" the pirates and threatened to "have my [Dyre] brains beat out or a stab for seizing the said ship." Shrimpton then sheltered the vessel at Noddles Island, "the place and receptacle of all piratical and uncustomed goods," and "received clandestinely great quantities of their gold, silver, jewels, and cacao."[124]

Despite King James II's best efforts to establish absolute control, both at home and abroad, he turned out to be his own worst enemy. In October 1687, the king issued a proclamation against pirates that more or less reiterated earlier proclamations about piracy being a "great detriment of Trade." But James II further alienated the colonists when he added that piracy was also "a prejudice of the Subjects of Our good Brother the Catholick King" of Spain.[125] Much like previous anti-piracy pronouncements, this one was just as ineffective, largely because the crown gave sole authority to convict or pardon pirates both at sea and in the colonies to a single person. James II selected Sir Robert Holmes to be the exclusive suppressor and prosecutor of pirates. The problem was that Holmes couldn't be everywhere at once, meaning it was impossible for him to suppress piracy over the entire Atlantic world. Even Edward Randolph found the proposition ridiculous and untenable.[126] In a letter to William Blathwayt, a member of the Privy Council in charge of colonial administration, Randolph expressed his frustration at having no authority of his own to assist in the suppression of pirates. He described the recent arrival of pirates into Rhode Island "with a large booty of Spanish plate" worth £70,000 to £80,000, which would have been a "good opportunity to make my fortune upon a Surrender of these pyrates." But because the proclamation focused on apprehending individual pirates instead of asserting authority over the colonies and communities that supported them, "wee must play at small games" during which "all will be lost for want of a tymely proceeding."[127]

Things continued to get worse for the king after he issued his Declaration of Indulgence in 1687, which not only suspended the penal laws for those unwilling to conform to the Church of England but also sought to undermine the Test Act of 1673 by no longer requiring a religious oath to be eligible for employment in government office. When several bishops, including the archbishop of Canterbury, petitioned King James II to reconsider the declaration, he had them arrested and tried on the charge of seditious libel. The following year, those who once saw James II's Catholic policies as a temporary nuisance now faced the possibility of a permanent Catholic dynasty when Queen Mary gave birth to a son, James Francis Edward, giving King James II a legitimate heir.

But behind the scenes, a group of Protestant noblemen had been negotiating with James II's Protestant daughter, Mary, and her husband, William of Orange, to come to England with a show of military force and seize power. When William and Mary arrived in November 1688, they were supported by many in James II's court and even his other daughter, Anne. In what became known as the Glorious Revolution, James II ultimately fled to France, where King Louis XIV afforded him protection and financial security. Parliament declared that James II had essentially abdicated when he threw the Great Seal of the Realm into the River Thames, and therefore Mary was now queen. Agents from Massachusetts happened to be in London during this transfer of power pursuing the restoration of the colony's charter and an end to the Dominion of New England. Rumor of the Glorious Revolution had spread to the colonies before official news was released, emboldening colonists to revolt. In April 1689, Bostonians overthrew the Andros regime, and the Dominion was dissolved. This is the political turmoil that Samuel Bellamy was born into in February 1689, which would significantly impact the opportunities available to him and, ultimately, his decision to turn pirate in 1716.

PART III

THE PIRATE ROUND
(CIRCA 1690–1714)

Chapter 5
THE NINE YEARS' WAR (1688—1697)

No man is a pirate unless his contemporaries agree to call him so.
—Samuel Taylor Coleridge[128]

The ascension of William and Mary to the throne during the Glorious Revolution may have been relatively bloodless, but the same could hardly be said about the first decade of their reign. King Louis XIV of France had, by 1678, become perhaps the most powerful monarch in Europe, giving him a sense of security as he aggressively annexed territories to fortify the French frontier. European Protestants grew increasingly alarmed, making William's new position as English king even more important. Now as both King William III of England and Stadtholder of the Dutch Republic, William III spearheaded an anti-French coalition known as the Grand Alliance between the English, Dutch, and the Holy Roman Empire. With war raging once again, pirates found ways to make themselves indispensable.

KING WILLIAM'S WAR: THE NORTH AMERICAN THEATER

In the American colonies, the Nine Years' War became known as King William's War, and the colonists were once more left to defend themselves in the absence of the crown's military support. Pirates of the region were more than happy to don their caps as privateers and protect the shipping to and from the colonies, especially in New England. When several French privateers appeared off the coast of New England in the summer of 1690, colonists were petrified. Mainland New Englanders, especially in Newport, Rhode Island, had received word of recent attacks on several local islands. One French man-of-war and a sloop attacked Block Island, where the privateers plundered homes and tortured residents for information on hidden valuables. One man refused to tell the French privateers, who observed "by the signs on the floor, that chests and other things were lately removed," where his chests were. One of the privateers was so enraged that he grabbed a "piece of a rail and struck him on his head therewith, and in such fury that the blood instantly gushed out and ran on the floor." Another man, in a case of mistaken identity, was "used barbarously" by the privateers, who whipped him "in an unmerciful manner, to make him confess where his money was."[129]

The French privateers were then joined by two additional French vessels and headed to "Fisher's Island where they fell to killing cattle and burning houses" while another group of French privateers seized thirteen ships off the New England coast.[130] At that point, the governor's council of Rhode Island commissioned Captain Thomas Paine to pursue the French privateers and protect Newport Harbor. Commandeering a sloop, the *Loyal Stede*, Paine and his crew headed to Block Island for information about where the French were headed next. The men quickly caught up with the privateers and waged "a very hot sea-fight for several hours," during which time one of the French captains, "a very violent, resolute fellow…took a glass of wine to drink" and boasted he would board the English immediately or face "his damnation if he did not." Unfortunately for him, while he was mid-drink, a bullet tore through his neck, after which "he instantly fell down dead." After taking the night to regroup, one of the Frenchmen, Captain Pekar, allegedly found out they were being pursued by Paine, whom Pekar "had sailed together a-privateering, Paine captain, and Pekar his lieutenant." Captain Pekar was heard saying that he would "as soon choose to fight with the devil as with him [Paine]" and fled, leaving Paine and his men to return to Newport.[131]

Rhode Island's governors, John Easton (1690–95) and Walter Clarke (1696–98), had no problem providing letters of marque to any and all privateers for the protection of the tiny colony and the benefit of their own pockets. Edward Randolph frequently complained about Clarke and Clarke's relatives to the Lords of Trade and Plantations. Randolph recounted one instance when "eight pirates came in from Fishers' Island (belonging to Connecticut) with a great deal of money and East India commodities, which

A depiction of the Battle of Cape Lopez between Captain Chaloner Ogle of HMS *Swallow* and Black Bart Roberts of the *Royal Fortune*, painting by Charles Edward Dixon, before 1934. *Wikimedia Commons*.

they brought from Madagascar in their brigantine." When HMS *Fowey*, on counter-piracy patrol along the North American coast, arrived in Rhode Island Harbor, Governor Clarke enabled six of the pirates to make their escape to Boston "with a great quantity of goods and money." In a show of good faith, the governor did seize two of them, George Cutler and Robert Munday, along with "about £1,400 or £1,500 in silver and gold taken from them." The pirates had not been in prison more than two days when they were released on bail, which had been secured by "Gresham Clarke, one of the Governor's uncles." According to Randolph, the two pirates took this opportunity to flee, "leaving their money to be shared by the Governor and his two uncles, who have been very great gainers by the pirates which have frequented Rhode Island." Further, he noted that "three or four vessels have been fitted out from thence to the Red Sea" by which the Clarke family "have enriched themselves by countenancing pirates." Even the deputy governor, John Greene, was in on the scheme, granting a commission to "one of the pirates who went to the Red Sea, without any security given by the master." Greene had previously been accused of being too liberal in his granting of privateering commissions by Nathaniel Coddington, who noted that Greene commissioned no fewer than thirty privateers in 1694 alone.[132]

Thomas Tew, the Rhode Island Pirate

By the end of the 1690s, the most infamous pirates of the Pirate Round era had caused immense damage to trade in the Indian Ocean. And their attacks proved to be a political nightmare for the English East India Company, its investors, and the crown. The English government ramped up its anti-piracy efforts, passing An Act for the More Effectuall Suppressions of Piracy in 1698.[133] The crown desperately needed to figure out the best approach for eradicating piracy in the kingdom's far-flung colonies. William Popple, secretary of the Board of Trade, realized that they needed detailed information about the colonists' activities from people with boots on the ground. So, Popple turned to one of the most zealous anti-pirate officials in the colonies, Jeremiah Basse, governor of East and West Jersey. Popple wanted to know which colonies were the most to blame for enabling the proliferation of pirates, details about the pirates and their abettors, and where the pirates were expected to return. He also asked Basse what court was available in either of the Jersies that "can or ever did try Pyrats," what laws they had authorizing them to do so, and what methods Basse thought "most proper to be used for the Suppressing of Pyrats."[134]

According to Basse, "Most of the Colonies of America" were "somewhat to blame in respect to their conduct towards" pirates, although for different reasons. Basse believed some of the colonies were simply ignorant of their duty while others were powerless to suppress the pirates. But to Basse, the most intolerable were those colonies that afforded the pirates protection because they were "no doubt blinded by the prospect of gaine & advantage." He told Popple that one of the colonies "most noted for protection or furnishings of them [the pirates]" was Rhode Island. Although the colony had developed a reputation as a refuge for debtors, dissenters, and fugitives (like pirates) early on, the exploits of the "Rhode Island Pirate," Thomas Tew, exposed the colony's complicity with pirates to the world. For Basse, there was one major reason why the crown had yet to eradicate piracy in the American colonies: the continued existence of private colonies. Pirates recognized, and took advantage of, the fact that the crown lacked authority over the governance of private colonies in New England. They felt secure in their belief that while they were being entertained in a private colony, the king did not have "suffitient power to seise them & bringe them to deserved punishment, which contributes not a little to their boldness."[135]

Thomas Tew was allegedly born to a prominent Rhode Island family. Evidence suggests that one of the colony's founders, Richard Tew, was his father and that Major Henry Tew, who once served as the colony's deputy governor, was his brother.[136] Many believe that Tew entered the maritime trade early. As an adult, he quickly made a name for himself sailing to and from the Indian Ocean several times on behalf of different colonial governors. Tew received his first privateering commission in 1691 while in Bermuda from Governor Isaac Richier. Richier charged Captain Tew and Captain George (on a second sloop) with seizing the French fort on Gorée, an island off the Senegalese coast, but the two sloops were quickly separated by a violent storm. With no word from their consort, Tew found the riches of the Mughal emperor to be a siren call. According to Captain Charles Johnson's account of Tew's exploits, Tew explained the situation at hand. Tew "was of Opinion, that they should turn their Thoughts on what might better their Circumstances," and should the crew be so inclined, Captain Tew "would undertake to shape a Course which should lead them to Ease and Plenty, in which they might pass the rest of their Days." If they succeeded, Tew believed "they might return home, not only without Danger, but even with Reputation." With a resounding cheer, the crew responded, "A gold Chain, or a wooden Leg, we'll stand by you!"[137]

The pirates changed course and made their way to the Strait of Babel Mandel, or Bab el-Mandeb, the narrowest point in the Red Sea.[138] Well known for carrying those making the hajj, or pilgrimage, from India to Mecca, the region was a prime hunting ground for pirates. Tew and his men would not be disappointed. Shortly after their arrival, the pirates saw a large, "richly laden" vessel followed by five additional ships that were "extreamly rich (one especially in Gold)." Tew's men were unsure that it was wise to attack this first ship considering it carried three hundred soldiers in addition to crew members. But Captain Tew told his men that they may be outnumbered and outgunned, but those soldiers did not have the two things necessary for success: "Skill and Courage." Tew's words proved true. He and his men easily boarded the ship without suffering a single loss. Apparently, the soldiers took "more Care to run from the Danger, than to exert himself in the Defence of his Goods." The pirates seized as much gold, silver, and jewels as they could manage as well as taking all the powder they could feasibly stow, throwing the rest of it overboard so it couldn't be used against them. This first haul earned each man upward of £3,000.[139]

In their early voyages on board the *Amity*, Captain Tew and his men did so well that they "commanded" the "cellar and servants, and committed debaucheries in" the "house and company" of New York's governor, Benjamin Fletcher. Reports indicate that Fletcher and Tew also "exchanged

The treasure chest of the Rhode Island Pirate, Thomas Tew, circa 1695, at the St. Augustine Pirate and Treasure Museum. Photograph by Carol M. Highsmith, 2020. *Courtesy of the Library of Congress.*

presents, such as gold watches." Although Tew had gained a reputation as "a man of infamous character, he was received and caressed by Governor Fletcher, dined and supped with him often, and appeared with him publicly in his coach."[140] Edward Randolph even alleged that Tew brought in no less than £100,000 to New York and Rhode Island.[141] Although this was likely exaggerated, at least £12,000 found its way into the coffers of Rhode Island governor Caleb Carr, and the majority of Newport residents were "enriched by" the loot brought home by Red Sea pirates like Tew.[142]

After amassing quite a fortune for himself, his crew, and his investors, Tew decided to settle back in Rhode Island. According to Johnson, Tew briefly lived quietly at home, unquestioned with his "easy Fortune." But the temptations of pirate life are great, and after being harassed by many of his former crew members, who had quickly squandered their share of plunder, to go pirating again in the Red Sea, Tew relented. In late 1695, Tew and the men made their way back to their old stomping grounds, where they pursued a convoy of twenty-five Mughal ships. Perhaps Tew should have stayed retired. When he and his crew attacked one of the vessels, "a Shot carried away the Rim of Tew's Belly, who held his Bowels with his Hands some small Space." The horrific sight allegedly "struck such a Terror in his Men, that they suffered themselves to be taken, without making Resistance," although they were later freed by Captain Henry Every.[143]

It would be Henry Every's actions that set into motion a major reconsideration of the value of piracy in the colonies. The trial of Every's men made New Englanders, in particular, very nervous. In a letter from the Board of Trade to Massachusetts Bay's lieutenant governor, William Stoughton, they reminded him that King William III had charged all colonial governors to "do their utmost to repress piracy." They also highlighted that during the trial of Every's crew, "there was too frequent mention of New England as the place from which pirates are fitted out and where they are entertained." According to one deposition, "all the pirates now out came from New England....They build their ships" and bring their pirate loot there, where New Englanders were able to make "a good estate that way." They ended their letter with a veiled threat, reminding Stoughton that "as we have given you orders to help your neighbour Colonies, so we have given them orders to help you in case of danger."[144]

Seeking to reassure the English government of Massachusetts Bay's anti-piracy attitude and lay blame elsewhere, some took matters into their own hands. Bostonian Benjamin Davis wrote to a London merchant named Edward Hull lamenting the colony's "sad posture for want...of help from the King."[145] He blamed King William III for allowing "so many petty governments," like Rhode Island, to continue on to the detriment of good colonies like Massachusetts. Further, he told Hull that there was "such a bloody crew of privateers at Rhode Island" that the local government could not control them, "and the sober men are in fear of their lives." These men were really pirates who were "daily plundering vessels as they come in," and unless King William III took some sort of action, they would ultimately govern the entire colony of Rhode Island.[146]

England was right to be wary of how the colonies handled issues of piracy. With the end of the Nine Years' War in September 1697, former privateers would be out of work and would most likely turn to (or return to) piracy to make a living. John Smith had recognized this conundrum nearly a century earlier: when the crown no longer needed privateers, "those [privateers] that were Rich" simply relied on what they had previously taken, while "those that

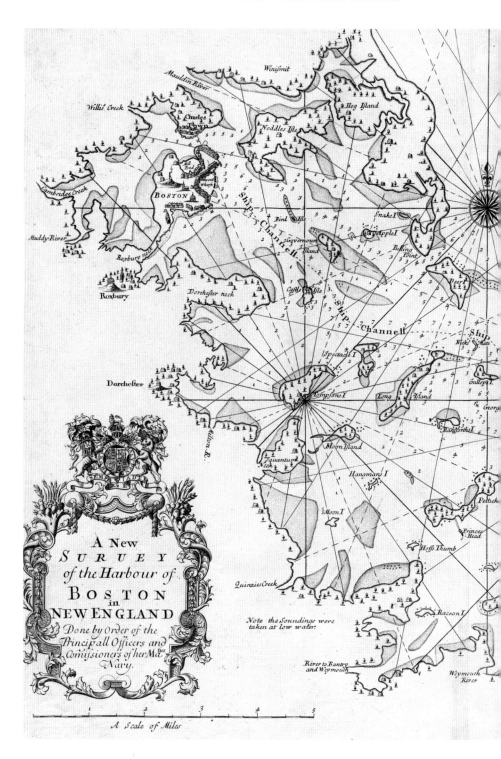

A New
SURVEY
of the Harbour of
BOSTON
in
NEW ENGLAND
Done by Order of the
Principall Officers and
Comissioners of her Maties
Navy.

Note the Soundings were
taken at low water.

A Scale of Miles

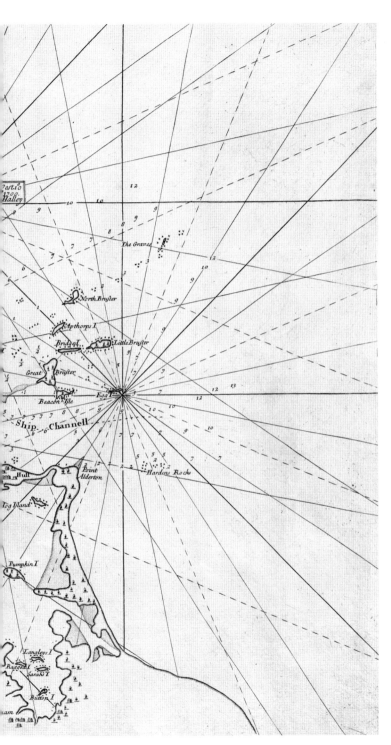

New survey of the harbour of Boston in New England, map, 1708. *Courtesy of the Mapping Boston Collection—Norman B. Leventhal Map & Education Center at the Boston Public Library.*

were poor and had nothing but from hand to Mouth, turned Pirates." And each person had their own reasons. According to Smith, "Some, because they became slighted of those for whom they had got much Wealth; some for that they could not get their Due; some that had lived bravely, would not abase themselves to Poverty; some vainly, only to get a name; others for Revenge, [or] Covetousness." As these individuals found themselves "more and more oppressed, their Passions increasing with discontent, made them turn Pirates."[147] So, what would Bellamy's reason be?

Chapter 6

THE WAR OF THE SPANISH SUCCESSION (1701–1715)

My advice to you, my violent friend, is to seek out gold and sit on it.
—the Dragon to Grendel[148]

By 1700, the existence of pirates coming from the North American colonies to plunder vessels in the Indian Ocean was practically nil. It seems that the crown and Parliament had developed a fairly effective multifaceted approach to eradicating piracy. By combining an aggressively anti-piracy Board of Trade, appointing anti-pirate government officials in the colonies, increasing naval presence in areas where pirates were known to hunt, passing new and loophole-free piracy laws, forcing alleged pirates to stand trial in England, offering risk-free pardons, and eliminating the economic enticement of Madagascar, the English government saw a pretty significant decline in piracy by around 1710. According to scholar Eric Jay Dolin, this top-down government approach was successful at reducing piracy, but the perspectives of those "on the ground" were more difficult to combat. Since many of these merchants, colonists, and local politicians had "long welcomed pirates into their midst as respected members of the community," they found it hard to suddenly reject them. George Larkin, a barrister in the High Court of Admiralty who was sent to New England to investigate and curb illicit trade, was surprised at how pirates were still "esteemed" as "very honest men." To give the members of the Board of Trade an indication of just how highly

A digital rendering of one of Black Bart Roberts's pirate flags, circa 1720, artist unknown, 2021. *Wikimedia Commons.*

esteemed the pirates could be among the local population, he told them about the upcoming nuptials between the daughter of "the President of the Council of New Hampshire, Secretary of the Province and Clerk of the inferior Court" and "one of these villains."[149]

While the crown and Parliament increased their collective effort to suppress piracy, a power vacuum in the Spanish Empire was created when King Charles II died without an heir apparent in November 1700. Two factions emerged. There were those who supported the ascension of Philip of Anjou because he was named the heir presumptive (despite being French) in his great-uncle King Charles II's will. And then there were those who wanted to seat Charles of Austria (whose claim rested on also being a member of the House of Hapsburg like Charles II). England was still in the Grand Alliance with the Netherlands and the Holy Roman Empire, so they sided with Charles of Austria.[150] Meanwhile, Spain and France rallied behind Philip of Anjou.

QUEEN ANNE'S WAR:
THE NORTH AMERICAN THEATER

The North American colonies were the theater of a subsidiary conflict during the War of the Spanish Succession called Queen Anne's War (1702–13). It was named for Queen Anne, who ascended to the throne upon the death of her brother-in-law King William III in 1702. New Englanders, along with their Indigenous allies, found themselves facing frequent raids into their towns by French colonists and their Indigenous forces. Additionally, French privateers based out of Acadia and Placentia harassed New England shipping and fishing.[151] Historians estimate that during the course of Queen Anne's War, French privateers took over one hundred prizes to Placentia alone. The war, which Anne had inherited, grew increasingly expensive and unpopular over the course of her reign.

And while she faced external conflict in the form of war, she also faced internal turmoil. The two-party political system became further entrenched during her reign, and the disagreements between Tories and Whigs grew increasingly hostile. She was confronted with betrayal by her closest friend and, much like her predecessors, struggled with religious quarreling. And after seventeen pregnancies (only five of which were live births, none surviving to adulthood), her health was in significant decline. She died on August 1, 1714, without an heir. Based on the Act of Settlement of 1701 banning Catholics from the line of succession, she was succeeded by George, Elector of Hanover, her closest living Protestant relative.[152] The question now was: would King George I maintain the anti-piracy crusade of his immediate predecessors?

JOHN QUELCH GOES ROGUE

It seems that during Queen Anne's War, piracy suddenly stopped appearing as a hot-button issue in government and merchant correspondence. By virtue of being at war, many of these former or would-be pirates had two equally appealing options. First, they could join the ranks of the Royal Navy, which increased its numbers by thirty thousand personnel over the course of the war. Men were tempted by the fact that they could earn double what they might earn as a seaman in peacetime. The other option was to join one of the over 1,600 privateering vessels, which held the promise of great riches.

But privateering commissions weren't as loose as they'd been in years past. And it was in this context that John Quelch, an English seaman operating out of Marblehead, Massachusetts, found himself on the wrong side of a letter of marque.

In the summer of 1703, several prominent citizens and merchants from Boston pooled their finances and resources to outfit a privateer. Sir Charles Hobby, Colonel Nicholas Paige, John Colman, William Clarke, and Benjamin Gallop hoped to take advantage of the war. The men purchased a brigantine, *Charles*, and named Captain Daniel Plowman its commander. The vessel's owners then convinced Joseph Dudley, governor of both Massachusetts and New Hampshire, to issue Captain Plowman a letter of marque so that he and his crew could attack enemy ships near Acadia and Newfoundland. Sir Charles Hobby contradicts this account of events in a 1705 letter to the Board of Trade in which he states that it was Governor Dudley who approached *him* with the idea to fit out his brigantine, the *Charles*, as a privateer.[153] Regardless, the commission granted the privateers of the *Charles* license to "War, Fight, Take, Kill, Suppress and Destroy, any Pirates, Privateers, or other the Subjects and Vassals of France, or Spain…in what Place soever you shall happen to meet them."[154] Plowman also received additional instructions, which included requirements such as keeping a detailed record of their actions and making sure no prisoners, even if "known to be of the Enemies side," were "in cold Blood killed, maimed," or tortured contrary to the laws of war. Additionally, anything seized by the crew of the *Charles* was to first be brought to an admiralty court for judgment. If, and only if, the court determined their seizure to be a lawful prize, *then* the plunder could be divided among captain, crew, and ship owners.[155]

Plowman navigated the *Charles* from Boston to Marblehead for provisions and personnel, but at some point, between sailing and arrival, he became very ill. He wrote to Colman and Clarke to tell them he was daily growing "worse and worse," to the point of being physically incapable of taking the *Charles* on its intended voyage and implored them to come quickly and save what they could. The two owners immediately went to Marblehead, but Plowman was too sick to see them. Instead, he sent further word that they should have the *Charles* sent back to Boston, where they could have all items on board the ship landed "to prevent all manner of Imbezelments" and warned them not to let "any second Thoughts of a Voyage tempt you, for it will not do with these People." Plowman feared that if the owners chose a new commander, within "Three Months all [would be] totally lost," and they might all lose more than just their money.[156]

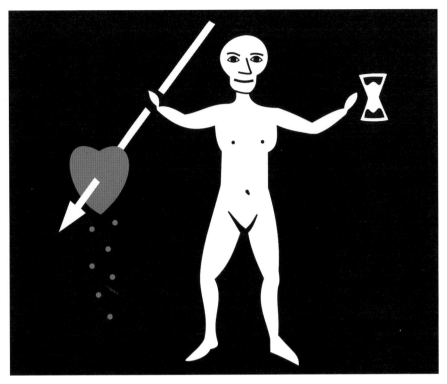

A digital rendering of the pirate flag associated with Captain John Quelch, circa 1703, by Orem, 2006. *Wikimedia Commons.*

While there is no record of Colman and Clarke's plans for moving forward, it appears they returned to Boston before giving any clear directions to the crew of the *Charles*. With the owners gone and Captain Plowman too ill to do anything, the men mutinied and locked Plowman in his cabin. When Quelch returned to the *Charles*, rather than confront the mutinous men, he joined them and assumed command of the ship. Instead of heading north toward Acadia and Newfoundland, the pirates made for the South Atlantic. Shortly after departing Marblehead, Plowman was thrown overboard, although the records do not indicate if he was alive at the time.[157]

The owners of the *Charles*, upon realizing that the ship had left Marblehead with Plowman in duress and believing the pirates intended to sail to the Caribbean, sent a letter to the governors of English colonies in the West Indies to warn them. In the letter they noted that they suspected Captain Plowman was dead, that the crew was "in Rebellion against their Officers," and that they feared the pirates' "design is not to do justly by us." In addition to trying to save their reputations, the vessel's owners were also evidently concerned about their financial investment. They informed the governors in the West Indies that, should the *Charles* come to one of their ports, the owners were to have "one Third of all Purchase[s]" for the ship and its provisions and fifty percent of the value of the small arms and ammunition on board. Additionally, Sir Charles Hobby was to be given the entire amount "proper for this Market" earned from the sale of two enslaved African men, Charles and Caesar, he had "loaned" to the crew. And the owners of the *Charles* were to receive the profits from the sale of an enslaved African boy named Mingo belonging to the presumed-dead Captain Plowman, which they would split among themselves.[158]

A Man with a Plan

But Quelch and the mutinous crew weren't headed for the islands in the West Indies. Instead, they made their way to Brazil, a Portuguese colony known for its rich gold deposits of mammoth proportions. Rumor had spread that Brazil's coastal defenses were weak, so the pirates hoped they would be able to easily seize and plunder the ships ferrying gold from the colony back to Portugal. And so began the brief piratical rampage of Quelch and his men. Around November 15, 1703, the pirates' first capture was a Portuguese fishing vessel from which they took "a quantity of Fish and Salt" valued at approximately £3. A few days later, they seized a small Portuguese brigantine, plundering five chests of Brazilian sugar worth £150 and six barrels of molasses worth £6. On or about November 24, Quelch and his men pillaged another small Portuguese brigantine, taking another five chests of Brazilian sugar worth £150 and a "quantity of Molasses, Rice, and Farine" valued at £10.[159]

In December, Quelch and his crew seized no fewer than four separate Portuguese ships of varying sizes. In total, they pillaged nearly £325 worth of goods, including rum, linen, silks, coinage, and sugar. Things went even better for the pirates from Marblehead when, on January 15, 1704, they captured a Portuguese brigantine from which they made away with £6,000 worth of gold dust and £900 of coined gold. A few weeks later, Quelch and his men took a Portuguese vessel, stealing over £130 in commodities and two hundred pieces of eight.[160] With prizes worth over £7,500, Quelch and the crew decided to head back to Marblehead. One of the men who was pressed into piratical service on board the *Charles*, Matthew Pymer, kept a detailed journal of their voyage. Quelch knew how damning this evidence would be and tore out five or six pages, which covered the period from October 1703 to February 1704, the exact time frame during which they "committed their Piracies." Additionally, Quelch ordered that all documents in Portuguese were to be thrown overboard and destroyed. According to Pymer's testimony, while refitting in Bermuda, Quelch coached the men on what to say upon returning to Marblehead. Their cover story for all their sudden riches was that, while on their privateering voyage, they "met with some Indians who had got great Treasure out of a Wreck" and took the gold from them.[161]

After the pirates returned to Marblehead, Quelch quickly made his way to Boston to meet with Colman and Clarke. Quelch told them the invented story about stealing gold from "Indians" at a shipwreck and gave them "their share" of the voyage in the form of several bags of coins and gold dust. The captain hoped this would appease the owners and keep them from asking any questions about the true nature of the voyage. But it was to no avail. Colman and Clarke were already wary of Quelch after the whole leaving-Marblehead-without-approval debacle, so his story was a flimsy cover at best. When the owners searched the *Charles*, their suspicions were confirmed. Despite their best attempts at destroying evidence against them, Quelch's men failed to conduct a thorough sweep of the ship. Colman and Clark found a number of Portuguese documents on board as well as a Portuguese flag. Even more damning was a bag of sugar containing Portuguese instructions for its delivery to Lisbon and the fact that most of the coins Quelch had given the owners were Portuguese. Recognizing that they would be considered accomplices subject to the same fate as the actual pirates, the owners immediately went to the secretary of Massachusetts Bay, Isaac Addington, to give a sworn statement about their observations.[162]

Lieutenant governor of the colony Thomas Povey immediately had Quelch and six of his men arrested on suspicion of piracy. The next day, Povey published an announcement in the *Boston News-Letter* listing the names of thirty-four additional men suspected of pirating with Quelch and requesting their speedy apprehension to facilitate examination of the accused in Boston. Povey further noted that the colonists were "strictly forbidden to entertain, harbour or conceal any of the said Persons, or their Treasure" and that they were not to "convey away, or in any manner further the Escape" of any of the suspected pirates. If they did, they would suffer the "utmost Severity of Law" and be charged as "accessories and partakers with

THE

Arraignment, Tryal, and Condemnation,

OF

Capt. John Quelch,

And Others of his Company, &c.

FOR

Sundry *Piracies, Robberies,* and *Murder,* Committed upon the Subjects of the King of *Portugal,* Her Majesty's Allie, on the Coast of *Brasil,* &c.

WHO

Upon full Evidence, were found Guilty, at the *Court-House* in *Boston,* on the Thirteenth of *June,* 1704. By Virtue of a Commission, grounded upon the Act of the Eleventh and Twelfth Years of King *William,* For the more effectual Suppression of Piracy. With the Arguments of the QUEEN's Council, and Council for the Prisoners upon the said Act.

PERUSED

By his Excellency *JOSEPH DUDLEY,* Esq; Captain-General and Commander in Chief in and over Her Majesty's Province of the *Massachusetts-Bay,* in *New-England,* in *America,* &c.

To which are also added, some PAPERS that were produc'd at the Tryal abovesaid.

WITH

An Account of the Ages of the several Prisoners, and the Places where they were Born.

LONDON:

Printed for *Ben. Bragg* in *Avemary-Lane,* 1705.

(Price One Shilling.)

The title page of the published piracy trial transcript for Captain John Quelch and his crew, 1705. *Courtesy of the Library of Congress.*

them [the pirates] in their Crime."[163] Ultimately, after a couple of months of exhaustive searching, only about half of the pirates of the *Charles* were apprehended. The remainder of the men managed to escape, disappearing along with their share of the plunder. The trial lasted all of three days, and a total of nineteen of the pirates were convicted and sentenced to hang, including Quelch. The executions were to take place on June 30, 1704, leaving the men to contemplate their fates in a Boston jail for over a week. In the meantime, Governor Dudley decided that only seven of the men, Quelch included, would actually be executed, the rest being too young and ignorant to fully comprehend the severity of their actions. Those men later received pardons from Queen Anne.[164]

DEATH IS GREAT FOR THE APPETITE

On the day of the execution, the condemned men were marched from the jail to Scarlet's Wharf on the edge of Boston Harbor, a distance of approximately three-quarters of a mile. The grim procession was complete with two ministers, the provost marshal and his officers, and the town's constables, all of whom were guarded by a contingent of forty musketeers, as the path was "Crowded and thronged on all sides with Multitudes of Spectators." From the wharf, the men were taken by boat to the gallows at Hudson's Point, where upward of 150 vessels filled with curious onlookers sat on the Charles River. Even more people lined the hill leading to the gallows. The ministers admonished the condemned, born sinners who chose to live as sinners, for not taking their advice to repent and receive God's "Saving and Healing Hands."[165]

After the men were led onto the stage, one of the ministers offered prayer: that God would not let the condemned suffer to "continue in the Gall of Bitterness and Bond of Iniquity, and in the Possession of the Devil" and to "Knock off the Chains of Death which are upon their Souls." Further, concerned with the leering crowd, the minister prayed "that all the Spectators, may get Good by the horrible Spectacle that is now before them" and that any mariners among them "be Saved from the Temptations which do so threaten…[and] so ruine them!" Afterward, the prisoners were given a chance to offer their final words. Quelch was first and, according to observers, stated, "I am not afraid of Death, I am not afraid of the Gallows, but I am afraid of what follows." The ministers

An Account of the Behaviour and laſt Dying

SPEECHES

Of the Six Pirates, that were Executed on *Charles River*, *Boſton* ſide, on Fryday *June* 30th. 1704. *Viz.*

Capt. John Quelch, John Lambert, Chriſtopher Scudamore, John Miller, Eraſmus Peterſon *and* Peter Roach.

THE Miniſters of the Town, had uſed more than ordinary Endeavours, to Inſtruct the Priſoners, and bring them to Repentance. There were Sermons Preached in their hearing, Every Day : And Prayers daily made with them. And they were Catechiſed ; and they had many occaſional Exhortations. And nothing was left, that could be done for their Good

On Fryday the 26th. of *June* 1704. Purſuant to Orders in the Dead Warrant, the aforeſaid Pirates were guarded from the Priſon in *Boſton*, by Forty Muſketeers, Conſtables of the Town, the Provoſt Marſhal and his Officers. &c. with Two Miniſters, who took great pains to prepare them for the laſt Article of their Lives. Being allowed to walk on Foot through the Town, to Scarlets Wharff ; where the Silver Oar being carried before them ; they went by Water to the Place of Execution, being Crowded and thronged on all ſides with Multitudes of Spectators. ' The Miniſters then Spoke to the Malefactors, to this Effect.

' We have told you often, ye we have told you Weeping, That you have by Sin undone your ſelves ; That you were born Sinners, That you have lived Sinners, That your Sins have been many and mighty ; ' and that the Sins for which you are now to Dy, are of no common aggravation. We have told you, That there is a Saviour for Sinners, and we have ſhewn you, how to commit your ſelves into His Saving and Healing Hands. We have told you, That if He Save you, He will give you an Hearty Repentance for all your Sins, and we have ſhown you how to Expreſs that Repentance. We have told you, What Marks of Life, muſt be deſired for your Souls, that you may Safely appear before the Judgment Seat of God. ' Oh ! That the means uſed for your Good, may by the Grace of God be made Effectual. We can do no more, but leave you in His Merciful Hands !

When they were gone up upon the Stage, and Silence was Commanded, One of the Miniſters Prayed, as followeth.

The Prayer made by One of the Miniſters, after the Malefactors were firſt upon the Stage. [As near as it could be taken in Writing in the great Croud.]

O Thou moſt Great and Glorious LORD! Thou art a Righteous, and a Terrible GOD. It is a Righteous and an Holy Law that thou haſt given unto us. To break that Good Law, and Sin againſt thy Infinite Majeſty, can be no little Evil. Thy Word is alway True ; and very Particular, that Word of thine which has told us and warn'd us, *Evil Purſueth Sinners*. Here is a Number of men that have been very Great Sinners, and that are to Dy before their Time, for their being wicked overmuch. God knows the Prayers, the Pains, the Tears, and the Agonies that have been Employ'd for them. And now, the Laſt Thing that we have to do for them, is to pour out with Anguiſh of Soul, our Prayer on their behalf ; Our Prayer, unto that God, with whom there is Mercy and Plenteous Redemption ; to that God, who is Rich in Mercy and Ready to Pardon. But how can we make our Prayer, without a Rapturous Adoration, of that Free-Grace, which has diſtinguiſhed us ! We, even we alſo, have every one of us an horrible Fountain of Sin in our Souls. There are none of the Crimes committed by theſe Miſerable Men, or by the worſt of thoſe Criminals that go down into the Pit, but we find the Seeds of them, in that Original Corruption, which we brought into the World with us. If God had left us to our ſelves, as He juſtly might have done, there is not the beſt among us

all, but what would ſoon have done the worſt things in the World. Oh ! The Free-Grace ! Oh ! The Free-Grace ! Oh ! The Riches of that Grace, which has made all the Difference ! But now, we Cry mightily to Heaven, we Lift up our Cries to the God of all Grace, for the Periſhing Souls which are juſt now going to Expire under the Stroke of Juſtice, before our Eyes. We Mourn, we Mourn, that upon ſome of them at leaſt, we do unto this Minute ſee no better Symptomes. But, Oh ! is there not yet a Room for Sovereign Grace to be diſplay'd, in their Converſion and Salvation ! They Periſh, if they do not now Sincerely Turn from Sin to God, and give themſelves up to the Lord JESUS CHRIST ; They Righteouſly, and Horribly Periſh ! And yet, without Influences from above, they can do none of thoſe things, which muſt be done, if they do not periſh. Oh ! Let us beg it of our God, that He would not be ſo Provoked, at their Multiplied and Prodigious Impieties, and at their obſtinate Hardneſs under means of Good formerly afforded them, as to withold thoſe Influences from them ! We cry to thee, O God of all Grace, That thou wouldeſt not Suffer them to continue in the Gall of Bitterneſs and Bond of Iniquity, and in the Poſſeſſion of the Devil. Oh ! Knock of the Chains of Death which are upon their Souls ! Oh ! Snatch the prey out of the Hands of the Terrible. Yet once again ! Once more ! We bring them, and lay them before the Spirit of Grace. O Almighty Spirit of Grace, May theſe Poor, blind, and Sinners, become objects for the Triumphs of Grace ! O Almighty Spirit of God, and of Grace ; cauſe theſe poor men to ſee their own Sinfulneſs and Wretchedneſs ! Make them Willing to be Saved from ſuch Sinfulneſs and Wretchedneſs

Diſcourſe

The title page from a published account of the behavior and final words of Captain John Quelch and his condemned crew members, 1704. *Courtesy of the Library of Congress*.

did not believe him, especially after he took off his hat and bowed to the spectators, "not behaving himself so much like a Dying man." Rather than take any responsibility, Quelch also used his final moments to say, "I forgive all the World" and everyone should "take care how they brought Money into New-England, [they might] be Hanged for it!" The remaining men—John Lambert, Christopher Scudamore, John Miller, Erasmus Peterson, and Peter Roach—mostly pleaded their innocence, appeared penitent, and expressed concern for their souls. Peterson went so far as to consider the whole thing farcical, remarking, "It is very hard for so many mens Lives to be taken away for a little Gold." The seventh man, Francis King, was spared at the last moment by Governor Dudley and ultimately received the queen's pardon. According to Samuel Sewall, secretary of Massachusetts Bay and acting chief justice of the Superior Court, when the "Scaffold was let to sink, there was such a Screech of the Women" in the audience that his wife heard it from their home a full mile from the execution site. Afterward, according to the "barbarous custom of the times," the deceased pirates' bodies were left "hanging on the gibbet until, by decay or the attacks of birds of prey, they gradually disappeared."[166]

After the execution of these pirates, the Council and Assembly of Massachusetts Bay hoped their actions would satisfy Queen Anne and Parliament. In a letter to the queen, they noted their "just resentment and detestation of the piracys and robberies" committed by Quelch and his crew and that they "hope the speedy justice that has been done upon those vile criminals will vindicate the Government from the imputation of giveing any countenance to, or favouring of such wicked actions."[167] But not everyone was pleased with the outcome. The owners of the *Charles*, upon hearing of Quelch's fate, learned that the ship and its effects were considered forfeit. One of the owners, Sir Charles Hobby, wrote to the Board of Trade that the owners "at the request of the Governor and purely for the service of the country at their own charge fitted out the vessel" and that it would be a "very great hardship unless they have some compensation for their loss."[168] His letter went unheeded. Of what little treasure was recovered, approximately £750 went to covering the costs associated with the capture, imprisonment, trial, and execution of the pirates. The remaining treasure, approximately 788 ounces of gold, was sent to London, where it was inspected by the master of the Royal Mint, Sir Isaac Newton. Yes, *that* Sir Isaac Newton. Although the gold was found to be significantly contaminated with lead, the value was still calculated to be just over £3,100, much of which was used to pay off some of the debt from the War of the Spanish Succession.[169]

Quelch's trial is interesting for a few reasons. But one of the big reasons was that it was the first English Admiralty trial against piracy conducted outside of England and became the model by which justice would be meted out to pirates and their accomplices between 1714 and 1726. One nineteenth-century New England author remarked that Quelch's trial and its subsequent impact was "one of the clearest cases of judicial murder in our American annals."[170] Colonies once a safe refuge for pirates often found themselves under the leadership of anti-pirate royal governors who, as author Clifford Beal described, set up their own "pirate-prosecution factories."[171]

Quelch's trial also seemed like a contradictory sham after the British government passed the Cruisers and Convoys Act in 1708. Knee-deep in the economic devastation wrought by war, the British government sought additional private assistance through privateers. At the outset of the war, commissions were granted on the basis that the crown would receive 10 percent of whatever a privateer plundered. To further incentivize privateers, the government decided to eliminate the crown's share, leaving the value of the prize to be shared among the investors, captains, and crew. Additionally, the act declared that if a privateer captured an enemy warship, they would receive a bounty of five pounds per enemy mariner. While the act was spectacularly helpful militarily, British merchants were concerned about the disruption to their own trade and feared that once a declaration of peace was made, the act would effectively "leave to the world a brood of pirates to infest it."[172]

They were right to worry. It truly was a tale as old as time, but the stakes were now much higher, unleashing what Rediker refers to as a "dialectic of terror." Rediker further notes that no one at the time was surprised that, out of the complex array of economic and sociopolitical forces that emerged from the war, "would climb the pirate, with a dagger between his teeth."[173] To get a sense of just how dramatic this particular rise in unemployment was, between 1712 and 1714, the British Royal Navy went from nearly fifty thousand men to fewer than fifteen thousand. One of those men who found himself in the unemployment line after the War of the Spanish Succession ended was none other than Samuel "Black Sam" Bellamy. Bellamy entered a "wooden world" where mariners took part "in a profoundly collective work experience, one that required carefully synchronized cooperation with other maritime workers for the sake of survival." Such experience influenced the decision of men like Bellamy to go upon the account and how those pirates would conduct themselves.[174]

PART IV

DAMN THEM FOR A PACK OF CRAFTY RASCALS: BELLAMY ENTERS THE CHAT

Chapter 7

THE EARLY TRIALS AND TRIBULATIONS OF BLACK SAM

I scorn to do any one a Mischief, when it is not for my Advantage.
—*Samuel Bellamy* [175]

Bellamy decided to go to North America in the hopes of improving his fortunes, and it is there that he surfaces in the records, landing at Eastham, Massachusetts, in late 1714 or early 1715.[176] What or who influenced Bellamy's decisions after arriving in New England has been amiably debated for the last three centuries. I'll provide both folklore and matters in the historical record and let the reader decide for themselves what prompted Bellamy's fateful choice.

LOVE, LUST, OR LEGEND?

Legends about Maria Hallett, the so-called Witch of Wellfleet, are deeply ingrained in the history of Cape Cod. The story goes that Bellamy enjoyed himself a little too much at the tavern one night and passed out. The next morning, desperately trying to stave off a hangover, Bellamy ventured toward an orchard when he noticed a beautiful young girl with long blonde hair that "glisten[ed] like cornsilk at suncoming." The girl, age fifteen or sixteen years, was Maria Hallett. As she was resting beneath an apple tree, Bellamy approached her and looked deep into her stunning eyes—

She Would Sit Quite Still, Permitting Barnaby to Gaze, by Howard Pyle, 1896. *Wikimedia Commons.*

described by some as being "as yellow as her hair," with others claiming they were "as blue as the deeps of Gull Pond." The two "fell instantly in love." Another version says that after he left the tavern, Bellamy was bewitched by "angelic singing" and followed the voice until he came to an apple tree under which Maria sat, again immediately falling in love. Maybe it's the version in which, while enjoying a beverage in Higgins Tavern, Bellamy was staring despondently out the window when he noticed Maria in an orchard, falling in love at first sight. Regardless of how (or even *if*) they met, legend has it that they talked for many hours. And by "talked," I mean that Bellamy "made masterful love, sailorman love that remembers how a following wind falls short and makes way while it blows" to Maria, the teen "full of virginity and youth."[177]

There are as many stories about who Maria Hallett was as there are about Samuel Bellamy's origins, but most who believe Maria existed believe that she was most likely the daughter of John Hallett, a successful local farmer. This sets up the two as star-crossed lovers: the poor, lowly English sailor and the (relatively) wealthy daughter of a prominent New Englander. According to the local lore, Bellamy and Maria spent several months together, inseparable. But Bellamy knew Maria's parents would never allow her to marry him while he was a penniless sailor, so he made Maria a promise that he would make his fortune and return to her. Some have gone so far as to embellish an already embellished tale, suggesting that Bellamy's final words to Maria were that upon his return, he "would wed her by ring…and in a sloop laden with treasure, carry her back to the Spanish Indies, there to be made princess of a Western Isle."[178]

Those who believe the legendary love story between Bellamy and Maria think that Bellamy's desire to marry Maria is what drove him to seek his fortune by diving at the recent wreckage of two Spanish treasure fleets off the coast of Florida.[179] Further, they use Bellamy's actions in the spring of 1717 as evidence supporting the existence of the relationship and his initial motives for going to sea. Although there is no significant corroborating documentation for the lovers, Bellamy did truly leave Massachusetts to become fabulously wealthy by diving the Spanish fleets' wreckage. So, how did a penniless sailor plan to sail the roughly 1,500 nautical miles from Cape Cod to Florida?

You've Got a Friend in Me

With no money and no real connections in Eastham, in the summer of 1715 Bellamy headed to Boston, where he met a successful silversmith named Paulsgrave Williams.[180] Williams was a thirty-nine-year-old married father of two and hailed from a well-respected New England family. His grandfather Nathaniel Williams had served as a lieutenant in the colonial militia of Massachusetts Bay and worked as a constable in Boston. He managed to build a fairly large estate in Boston. Paulsgrave Williams's father, John Williams, was a successful merchant and attorney general of Rhode Island. The family split their time between their mansion in Boston and their estates in Newport and Block Island. His mother, Ann Alcock Williams, was the daughter of a highly respected physician and was closely related to the principal founders of Block Island and Charlestown, Massachusetts. Paulsgrave Williams hardly seems the type of person one might expect to choose to suddenly turn to a life of piracy. But circumstances shaped Williams's life and ultimately impacted Bellamy's in unexpected ways.[181]

Williams's father died when he was just eleven years old. His mother quickly remarried, choosing the family's legal executor, Robert Guthrie, as her new husband. Guthrie was a Scottish exile and moved in very different circles than the Williams family. Williams was introduced to the wide world of illicit commerce in New England, including money laundering, smuggling, and running underground markets. And it soon became a family affair. Williams's older sister, Mary, wed Edward Sands, who was one of Captain Kidd's close friends. The pair were said to have concealed some of Kidd's wealth while he evaded the authorities. And Williams's younger sister, Elizabeth, married another of Kidd's friends named Thomas Paine. Paine was the nephew of the aforementioned retired pirate Thomas Paine who, in his later years, switched from plundering the vessels to buying and selling goods that had already been plundered. Elizabeth and her husband were even implicated in assisting Kidd while he was on the run.[182]

So it was that Williams and Bellamy realized the opportunity before them. Between Bellamy's seafaring skills and Williams's power and money, the two felt they would become an unstoppable force. The two had just bought a ship when news reached Boston about two Spanish treasure fleets, the *Nueva Españo* and the *Tierra Firme* fleets, which were wrecked in a hurricane off the coast of Florida. In total, eleven Spanish ships were lost,

A southeast view of the great town of Boston in New England in America, engraving by John Carwitham, circa 1730. *Courtesy of the New York Public Library.*

from which over seven hundred men died. Due to the recent war, which made ferrying Spanish treasure from the Americas to Spain much more dangerous, the ships contained a significantly larger amount of cargo than they would normally carry. Reports indicated that the wreckage contained over fourteen million pieces of eight. This was it: a chance for Bellamy, sailor of Plymouth, to show his quality![183]

With Bellamy as captain and Williams as quartermaster, the two put together a small crew for the purpose of salvaging what they could from the sunken Spanish ships. But by the time the men reached the wreck site in January 1716, nearly six months had passed since the fleets went down. Everyone and their mother had flocked to the scene hoping to claim some of the vast treasure lying on the ocean floor. They would all be disappointed. The Spanish government had begun salvaging immediately after the storm and had secured the area to prevent interlopers. But the trip to the wreck site wasn't a total loss for Bellamy and Williams. In fact, it was a small bump in the road to glorious riches.

No Honor Among Thieves

After realizing that the wreck site was a bust, Bellamy and Williams headed to the Bay of Honduras to determine their next move. Meanwhile, several members of the Flying Gang, a loose coalition of pirates operating out of Nassau on Providence Island in the Bahamas, had tried their hand at salvaging the wreckage, too. But they found it more fruitful to let others do the hard work and then raid the ships and campsites of the salvage divers. That, of course, didn't last long. Soon, Bellamy and Williams would find themselves introduced and adopted into this Flying Gang, altering the course of their pirating. But first, they had to get their feet wet.

When Williams and Bellamy arrived at Campeche in southeastern Mexico, they decided their best bet would be to officially go on the account. They sold their ship and used the money to purchase two periaguas, which could carry upward of thirty men each.[184] And it turned out they had a group of willing and eager recruits for their pirating venture. While in Campeche, Bellamy and Williams encountered some English loggers—also known as Baymen—whose illegal camp had been assaulted by the Spanish militia. These survivors feared additional Spanish raids and saw Bellamy's scheme as a means of escape. With new vessels and an expanded crew, it was time to make their mark.

The first boat Bellamy and his crew seized was captained by John Cornelison.[185] While it's unclear what exactly they plundered from the ship, perhaps the most valuable was a seaman named Peter Cornelius Hoof.[186] A Swedish mariner, Hoof had spent the previous eighteen years sailing primarily for the Dutch in and around the Caribbean and South America; thus, he brought considerable navigational knowledge to Bellamy's crew. According to Hoof, he had no choice in the matter, as "Bellamy's Company Swore they would kill him unless he would joyn with them in their Unlawful Designs."[187] Hoof once tried to run shortly after being pressed into service but was severely whipped for his transgression. While successful, their first few captures were relatively inconsequential. But while they sailed off the coast of Cuba, Bellamy and his boisterous crew caught the eye of the privateer-turned-pirate Henry Jennings.

Jennings, who captained the *Barsheba*, was at that time joined by Captain Leigh Ashworth in command of the *Mary*. Jennings and Ashworth followed Bellamy and Williams to the area of Bahía Honda on the northwestern coast of Cuba. Upon their initial meeting, it is said that the four were immediately friendly and spent a short time careening their

Walking the Plank, by Howard Pyle, 1887. *Wikimedia Commons*.

vessels before they caught sight of a French frigate, the *St. Marie*, not far in the distance.[188] The foursome agreed to work in concert to seize the ship and then divide the prize equally. In his deposition, Allen Bernard (Jennings's quartermaster) recalled being informed of the attack by one of his crewmates. He was told that Bellamy and Williams took the lead, deciding on a unique tactic to distract (or terrorize?) the Frenchmen. The crews of both men took off all of their clothing and, wearing nothing but their ammunition boxes, cutlasses, and pistols, approached the *St. Marie* in their periaguas. According to the man who relayed the attack to Bernard, "he had never seen such a sight before."[189]

According to one French account, however, the *St. Marie* had actually anchored nearby so the crew could gather wood and water. It was then that they were "attacked by five English Sloops and Two Peraguas under English Colours." After the pirates "Tormented the Crew to that Inhumane degree" to find out what money the Frenchmen had hidden on shore, the prisoners revealed where the pirates could find approximately thirty thousand pieces of eight and told them that the ship was also "very rich in Merchandize."[190] Regardless, the pirates were firmly in control of the *St. Marie*, its rich cargo, and a boatload of silver. While they relished in their success, the pirates learned that a French merchant ship, the *Marianne*, was trading nearby in Porto Mariel with a cargo valued at around fifty thousand pieces of eight. Never satisfied, Jennings dispatched some of his small pirate fleet to capture the vessel. But Jennings's men were too late: the infamous Benjamin Hornigold, commanding the *Benjamin*, had beaten them there and seized the *Marianne* for his own pirate flotilla.[191] Jennings, infuriated by the mere thought of being outdone by his bitter rival, quickly prepared the *Barsheba* and *Mary* to chase after Hornigold, leaving a small contingent of men to watch over the *St. Marie*.[192]

If ever there was a golden opportunity for Bellamy and Williams, this was it. Not thinking twice about backstabbing Jennings, they pulled one of their periaguas alongside the *St. Marie* and easily secured the ship. Their crews quickly tossed at least 28,500 "and odd pieces of eight" into the periagua and bolted out of the bay, leaving behind their other periagua. When Jennings returned, having failed to catch up to Hornigold, and was informed that the money was gone, he immediately ordered Bellamy and Williams's abandoned periagua "cut to pieces."[193]

The Return of the Pirate Ship, illustration by C.J. Staniland and J.R. Wells, 1884. *Courtesy of the Hathi-Trust.*

Robin Hood Meets the Flying Gang

Amassing such a windfall with minimal effort was certainly exhilarating for Bellamy, Williams, and their crew. Not long after making their escape, the men met Hornigold for themselves and were quickly absorbed into the Flying Gang. The Flying Gang was really more of a loose coalition that was deeply divided, but it was a group of leading pirates who used Nassau on the island of New Providence as their base of operations.[194] The fact that Bellamy and Williams did Jennings dirty must have influenced Hornigold's attitude toward the men, as Bellamy was made captain of the *Marianne* shortly after they met. Bellamy remained something of a pirate admiral, maintaining authority over each of the captains. The evidence of what happened afterward is debatable, with two different versions of events.

In the examination of Jeremiah Higgins, in October 1715, he was a foremast man on a sloop named the *Blackett*, which was bound for the Florida wrecks. Before reaching the wrecks, however, he was kidnapped and pressed into service by Captain Hornigold. Higgins described how "for some time after [they all] consorted together…untill a quarrell happened among the Company" in the summer of 1716. Although Higgins didn't elaborate on the cause of the quarrel, he deposed that the pirates "gave the said Sloop *Benjamin* to the said Hornigold" who, along with some of the crew, departed. But Higgins, who was forced to remain aboard the *Marianne*, noted that Bellamy sailed about "from place to place" for a short time when they "met with another Pyrate sloop called the *Postillion*…[with] one Capt. La Boos Commander." "La Boos" was a former privateer named Olivier Levasseur, who was known as La Buse (The Buzzard).[195]

But according to the testimony of John Brown, he was sailing on a vessel ferrying logwood to Holland around the beginning of 1716 when the ship was taken by "two Piratical Sloops, one Commanded by Hornygold and the other by a Frenchman called Labous." Brown said that over the next four months, they captured several prizes, including a couple of Spanish brigantines. Although the Spanish refused to pay any ransom for the ships, one of the crew members, a twenty-five-year-old Dutch mixed-race man of African heritage named Hendrick Quintor, joined the pirates.[196] The unlikely allies seemed to work well together, but the honeymoon was short-lived. With rare exception, Hornigold refused to attack and plunder English ships, still operating under the anti-French, anti-Spanish mindset of the recent war. Plus, it gave him that thin veneer of privateering legality. This refusal became such a point of contention among the crews that, by August

1716, "a difference arising amongst the English Pirates" had created a deep divide. The pirates held a vote among the collective crews and appointed Bellamy as commander of the pirate fleet. But the "difference" was hardly a mutiny, and Hornigold was free to leave in his sloop, the *Benjamin*, along with twenty-six of his most loyal supporters.[197]

THE FAIRLY ODD COUPLE

Regardless of when La Buse entered the picture, it seems that there was at least *some* honor among thieves. Hornigold probably made his way back to Nassau to gather new recruits and refit his sloop, but his pirating days weren't over just yet. Meanwhile, Bellamy and La Buse spent the next five months wandering aimlessly from Cuba to the Windward Islands and everywhere in between. They took countless vessels during their short run together, but from the records it appears that one of the pair's earliest captures was the *Elizabeth* in late summer 1716. The *Elizabeth* was just one of the many ships launched from Jamaica to fish the Spanish wrecks. Bellamy and La Buse "took out some provisions and Liquors," pressed several crew members into service (including the ship's master, Richard Caverley), and then sent the *Elizabeth* with its remaining crew on their merry way. Around the same time, they seized several canoes, periaguas, and lighters carrying "Bread pork Beeff and a few Fowls." After relieving the crews of their delicious cargo, they "sent them away about their" business.[198]

Food and provisions are good, and necessary, prizes, but they're not remotely the same kind of treasure as gold and silver. In late September or early October 1716, while off the coast of Puerto Rico, Bellamy and La Buse attempted to attack a French ship of about forty or forty-four guns. But after nearly an hour, with one man dead and four others wounded, the pirates were forced to quit and move on. Their next target was a French prison ship from which they took seven men, including Simon Van Vorst of New York and Thomas Baker, a Dutch tailor. Why were these two men on a prison ship? The prison ship was transporting many accused smugglers, so perhaps they were among that population. It may explain why Bellamy and La Buse would want to keep them in their fold. The pirates carried on.[199]

In early November 1716, Bellamy and La Buse were cruising between St. Thomas and St. Croix when they met with a sloop called the *Bonetta*, captained by Abijah Savage. The *Bonetta* had nearly completed its nearly one-thousand-nautical-mile journey from Jamaica to Antigua when, just after six o'clock in the morning, they saw the pirates. Savage, of course, attempted to flee. Nearly six hours later, after the world's slowest high-speed chase, the pirates caught up to the *Bonetta* and "fired a Cannon Ball" toward the ship. When Savage saw La Buse raise a "Black Flag," he immediately "struck his sails, hoisted out his Boat, and went on board them [the pirates]." Savage, his crew, and passengers were detained for about two weeks, during which time the pirates continued to hunt the waters, taking a "French Ship and six sail of small vessels all of which (after taking from them what they thought convenient) they discharged." Ultimately, Bellamy and La Buse decided to release the *Bonetta* and its passengers, but not before "taking from them several of their cloaths and other things particularly" an enslaved African man and Indigenous boy.[200]

The pirates may have gotten a little more than they bargained for, though, when Bellamy agreed to accept John King, a boy who couldn't have been more than ten or eleven years old, as a recruit. It wasn't unusual in the eighteenth century for young boys from poor families to hire themselves out as powder monkeys or cabin boys. But evidence suggests that King was from a family with money. According to Savage, King was a passenger on his sloop along with his mother, and travel by sail was not a cheap affair. A ticket (depending on distance) could cost upward of £5, the equivalent of nearly $1,300 today.[201] Seeming to corroborate this is the fact that, during archaeological excavations of the *Whydah* shipwreck site, Barry Clifford and his team found "a small shoe, a silk stocking and a small fibula, or lower leg bone." After showing the leg bone to the team's archaeologist, John de Bry, and an expert from the Smithsonian Institution, David Hunt, both agreed that the fibula was consistent with belonging to a child between eight and eleven years old. Examination of the stocking showed it to be woven French silk, and the shoe was "of upper-class design and craftsmanship."[202] Perhaps it was the boy's feisty attitude that led Bellamy to believe that King might prove useful on his pirate ship. King was *so* adamant about joining Bellamy's crew that Savage recalled that the boy "was so far from being forced or compelled" by the pirates, made abundantly clear by the fact that King "declared he would Kill himself if he was Restrained, and even threatned his Mother" if she tried to stop him.[203]

The following month turned out to be quite successful for the growing pirate gang. In early December 1716, the pirates decided to careen at St. Croix. While there, three of the pressed men attempted to run away. One of those was the aforementioned Peter Hoof, who, after "being brought back was severely whipped." After a brief stay, the pirates then headed windward to cruise "for what they could get."[204] They didn't have to search for long. Bellamy and La Buse soon came across a pair of ships on their way to the Bay of Campeche. One of the ships was the *Pearl*, led by Captain Tosor. The other was a twenty-six-gun merchant ship, *The Sultana*, commanded by Captain Richards. Although the pirates at that point had a record of generally taking goods and people from a vessel and returning the ship to the captain, Bellamy took a shining to *The Sultana*. It was larger and decidedly more powerful than the *Marianne*. The pirates looted the *Pearl*, taking what they could, and then put the crew of *The Sultana* on board the *Pearl*, keeping *The Sultana* for themselves. After a quick vote, it was decided that Bellamy would take command of *The Sultana*, while command of the *Marianne* was handed off to his longtime partner in crime, Paulsgrave Williams.[205]

Not long after the capture of *The Sultana* and the *Pearl*, the pirates sighted the *St. Michael* about twenty leagues off the coast of Saba.[206] Commanded by James Williams, the *St. Michael* had left Bristol in September bound for Jamaica. After holding the *St. Michael*'s crew hostage until January 9, 1717, the pirates returned the vessel to its captain, but not before seizing its cargo of salted pork, grains, cured beef, and other provisions. The pirates also pressed four of the *St. Michael*'s men into service. One of those men was the very valuable (and unmarried) Thomas Davis, a carpenter. According to the testimony of one of Davis's shipmates from the *St. Michael*, when Davis begged to be released, Bellamy put his fate to the vote of the pirate crew. The pirates "expressed themselves in a Violent manner, saying, 'No, Damn him,' they would first shoot him or whip him to Death at the Mast."[207] It was at this point that Black Sam and La Buse amicably parted ways. For Bellamy and Williams, their venture so far had proved most profitable, with at least fifty-two captures under their belt. They may have thought they'd seen the sun, but they hadn't seen it shine…yet. The best was yet to come.

Chapter 8

THE CURSE OF THE *WHYDAH*

They villify us, the Scoundrels do, when there is only this Difference, they rob
the Poor under the Cover of Law, forsooth, and we plunder the Rich under the
Protection of our own Courage.
—Samuel Bellamy [208]

While Sam Bellamy and Paulsgrave Williams had been busy making plans for fishing the Spanish treasure wrecks, a most impressive ship was being prepared in London—a ship that would ferry Bellamy not to riches or love but to an unexpected end. Commissioned in 1715 by London merchants specializing in the barbaric trafficking of enslaved Africans, the *Whydah* was formidable. A three-hundred-ton galley designed to carry over five hundred enslaved humans as well as a large store of gold, sugar, ivory, and other valuable goods, the *Whydah* could reach speeds nearing thirteen knots. The vessel also held eighteen guns standard, capable of carrying up to ten more when necessary.

The *Whydah*'s investors chose a longtime enslaver and trafficker, Lawrence Prince, to captain the vessel. Although Prince had gained some notoriety for his tactics and agents of the Royal African Company often complained that he undermined their operations by outbidding them, Prince was also known as a skilled seafarer and shrewd negotiator. The *Whydah* began its maiden voyage in early 1716. A typical slaving voyage in the early eighteenth century could take twelve or more months, depending on conditions. After sailing the *Whydah* from London to the slave coast of West Africa, Prince and his crew would probably have to wait several months before obtaining their captives. By the fall of 1716, negotiations were complete, and Prince forcibly carried his human cargo to the harbor in Kingston, Jamaica, where he barbarically auctioned the enslaved Africans and some of the other commodities the crew had picked up while in West Africa. Having left London nearly a year earlier, Prince and his fifty-man crew were ready to make the long trek home. They secured the cargo bound for London, including indigo, sugar, gold, and Jesuit's bark, and weighed anchor in the last week of February 1717.[209] But Captain Prince, a veteran seaman, was on high alert. This was, after all, the most dangerous leg of the triangle trade between Europe, Africa, and the Americas.

GOING QUICK DOWN INTO HELL

To get from Jamaica back to London, the *Whydah* had to sail through the heart of the pirate haunts before it reached the open Atlantic. This meant that Captain Prince needed to safely navigate between Cuba and Hispaniola and then through the Bahamas before he could confidently feel that the *Whydah* was home free. But the timing of their departure couldn't have been more fateful. As the *Whydah* was sailing between Cuba and Hispaniola in the Windward Passage, one of the crewmen informed Captain Prince that two vessels were rather closely following them. When Prince investigated, he saw the pair flying the Union Jack ensign and assumed they must be HMS *Adventure* and HMS *Swift*. But the closer they got, Prince began second-guessing himself. And when he saw the pair posture into an intercept course, he realized the danger the *Whydah* was truly in. The ships weren't Royal Navy vessels; they were pirates. Bellamy and Williams had their prey in sight. Experienced, Prince realized he needed to choose his next moves carefully. Pirates had a reputation for being more generous with captives who allowed them to seize a vessel's cargo unopposed. But if they chose to stand and fight, pirates would typically "give no quarter," meaning they would use all means necessary—including torture and murder—to get what they wanted.[210]

Prince decided on a middle-of-the-road course: he wouldn't immediately fire on the pirates, but he wasn't going to make the *Whydah*'s capture easy. He ordered more sail, and the crew did their best to evade *The Sultana* and the *Marianne*, forcing the pirates to chase the *Whydah*. The pirates "spread a large black Flag, with a Death's Head and Bones a-cross," and pursued the *Whydah* for three whole days, the pirates losing sight of the *Whydah* at one point. But the predators eventually ensnared their prey. Some of the pirates boarded the *Whydah*, and all three vessels were then anchored at Long Island.[211] According to the testimony of one of the men aboard Bellamy's flagship, there were around 120 pirates between *The Sultana* and the *Marianne*, meaning the crew of the *Whydah* were outnumbered at least two to one. Bellamy found the *Whydah* even more impressive and in better condition than *The Sultana* and, once again, decided to take a new flagship. But the pirates treated Prince and his crew rather civilly, offering them use of *The Sultana* to get back to London. For the next couple of weeks, the pirates busied themselves transferring their plunder from *The Sultana* to the *Whydah*. The pirates also shifted the cannons of *The Sultana* to the *Whydah*, increasing their firepower from eighteen guns to twenty-eight. Whatever cannons couldn't fit on the flagship were placed on the *Marianne*. But they gave Prince "as much of the best and finest goods" as "he desired," as well as about £20 in gold and silver "to bear his charges." Bellamy and his men kept the £20,000 to £30,000 they found in the *Whydah*. Accounts vary as to the number of men who abandoned the *Whydah* to join the pirates, ranging from seven to twelve, but one consistent fact was that all of those men were volunteers save the boatswain and two others.[212]

BELLAMY AND CAPTAIN BEER

It was now mid-March 1717, and the pirates had quite a "ship of force" to support their plundering. After allegedly holding a vote, the pirates decided they would make their way up the Eastern Seaboard of North America through the pirate nests of Charleston, the Chesapeake, New York, and all the way to the northern waters of Maine. Given that they would be traveling past his home on Block Island, Williams decided that he would stop on their way north to visit with his family and perhaps deliver his share of the plunder for safekeeping. It had, after all, been nearly two years since he'd last seen his loved ones. Bellamy and Williams decided that if they became separated at any point, they would find each other at Damariscove Island in Maine.[213]

Shortly after setting sail, the pirates came across a British merchant ship, the *Tanner Frigate*, which had recently departed from Petit Goave, the principal harbor of French Hispaniola. Under the command of John Stover, the ship was actually contracted out to the French and carried crew members from both nations. The *Tanner Frigate* was transporting a significant quantity of sugar back to France when the pirates attacked. One of the Englishmen on board, Thomas Checkley, deposed that Bellamy's crew "pretended to be Robbin Hoods Men" and that one of his crewmates, a French sailor named John Shuan, defected to the pirates most willingly. Checkley further testified that after Shuan "declared himself to be now a Pirate," he "went up and unrigged the Main top-mast by order of the Pirates" to prevent the *Tanner Frigate* from catching back up to the pirates upon release. Shuan also helped the pirates discover a hidden cache of 5,000 livres, which was roughly the equivalent of £375.[214]

After this latest catch, the pirates continued plying their way north, reaching the waters about forty leagues off the coast of South Carolina by early April. Here, they captured another recorded prize. Captain Beer, sailing from Block Island to South Carolina, had the great misfortune of crossing paths with the pirates. According to Beer's account, the *Marianne*, captained by Williams, kidnapped him. While on board, Beer identified Williams as also being from Block Island. In consort with Williams was "a very fine London built Galley of 30 guns, 200 brisk Men of Several Nations," which Beer noted was called the *Whydah*, being captained by Samuel Bellamy. Beer stated that he was held prisoner on board the *Whydah* for approximately two hours while the pirates plundered his ship. In his account, Captain Beer said that Williams was planning to return his ship, but the *Whydah*'s crew wanted to sink it instead.[215]

Captain Charles Johnson also describes the interaction between Captains Beer and Bellamy in his second volume of *The Pyrates*. A mix of fact and fantasy, the account still offers some interesting insight into this "Robin Hood" mentality that Bellamy had. Take the following conversation with a grain of salt, but I wanted to share the supposed political tirade that Bellamy went on while spending two hours with Beer. Bellamy first apologized to Beer, saying, "Damn my Blood, I am sorry they won't let you have your Sloop again, for I scorn to do any one a Mischief, when it is not for my Advantage." But Bellamy also blamed Beer for his own predicament, calling him a "sneaking Puppy" for submitting "to be governed by Laws which rich Men have made for their own Security." These rich men, in Bellamy's mind, were "cowardly Whelps [who] have not the Courage otherwise to defend what they get by their Knavery." Instead, they were "a Pack of crafty Rascals...Scoundrels" who vilify the pirates "when there is only this Difference, they rob the Poor under the Cover of Law, forsooth, and we plunder the Rich under the Protection of our own Courage."[216]

Bellamy then asked Beer why he would "sneak after the Asses of these Villains for employment" when it would be better for him to join the pirates, to which Beer replied that "his Conscience would not allow him to break thro' the Laws of God and Man." Enraged, Bellamy declared himself "a free Prince" with "as much Authority to make War on the whole World, as he who has a hundred Sail of Ships at Sea, and an Army of 100,000 Men in the Field."[217] Bellamy then sent Beer to the *Marianne*, where Williams agreed to take Beer back to Block Island with him.

Waves Crack with Wicked Fury

As the two pirate crews made their way north, they became separated off the coast of Virginia due to some difficult weather, which Richard Caverley, aboard the *Marianne*, described as "very foggy."[218] Having lost sight of the *Marianne*, Bellamy and the crew of the *Whydah* "cruised ten Days according to [the] agreement between" the pirate captains. During this period, they seized a number of prizes, even capturing three vessels in a single day. A sloop named the *Agnes* from Glasgow had recently departed Barbados bound for Virginia, "laden with Rum, Sugar, Molasses and sundry European goods." It was the first ship taken early in the morning on April 7, 1717, and "the greater part of the Cargo" was quickly seized by Bellamy and his crew. The pirates then took another ship from Glasgow, a one-hundred-ton snow called the *Anne Galley*, and a pink called the *Endeavor* from Bristol or Brighton.[219] According to the testimony of two men aboard the *Agnes*, the pirates found the sloop "too leaky" and, after plundering the ship, decided to sink it before proceeding further. A few days later, the pirates then took a ship from Leith. After taking what they wanted from both the *Endeavor* and the ship from Leith, they placed the crew of the *Agnes* aboard the *Endeavor* and released the two ships. But the pirates decided to keep the *Anne Galley* to help provide cover with the absence of the *Marianne*, placing eighteen of their own men aboard to join the *Anne Galley*'s crew of ten.[220]

Bellamy, now technically in command of three ships (the *Whydah*, *Marianne*, and *Anne Galley*), saw his ranks continuing to increase. Contemporary estimates of the number of men Bellamy had under his command range from 130 to over 200. Victims of the attack against the *Agnes* provided a description of the crew's ethnic makeup, testifying that "the greater part of the Pyrate's crew are natives of Great Britain and Ireland, the rest consisting of divers nations"

A depiction of the pirate Captain Edward "Ned" Low standing on shore during a hurricane, engraving from *History of Most Famous Highway Men* by Captain Charles Johnson, 1734. *Courtesy of the Library of Congress.*

as well as about twenty-five Africans that had been "taken out of a Guinea Ship." An anonymous letter to the Board of Trade also described the *Whydah*'s crew as "a Mix't Multitude of all Country's." The former prisoners also said that Bellamy's men informed them that the pirates intended to spend the next few weeks hunting Delaware Bay and Long Island Sound "to intercept some vessels from Philadelphia and New York bound with provisions to the West Indies." From there, the pirates would go to Green Island off the coast of Maine to careen their ships.[221] This information was corroborated by the deposition of John Brown, who was on board the *Whydah* at the time.

By late April, Williams and the men of the *Marianne* had reached Block Island, where they stayed a day or two. Williams spent some time visiting his mother and sisters, presumably making good on his plan to leave some of his plunder with his kin. Meanwhile, their proximity unbeknownst to them,

Bellamy and the men of the *Whydah* found themselves nearing the coast of Cape Cod. Legend has it that Bellamy planned to stop in Eastham to reunite with his beloved Maria Hallett, but the truth is lost to the sea. Regardless of *why* Bellamy was in the area, on April 26, 1717, the pirates noticed a pink called the *Mary Anne* of Dublin bound from Nantucket to New York. According to the testimonies of two men from the *Mary Anne*, Thomas Fitzgerald and Andrew Mackonochie, they were quickly encircled by the *Whydah* and *Anne Galley* and ordered to hoist their colors. After the captain of the *Mary Anne* did as told, the pirates "sent seven Men on board, Armed with their Musquets, pistols and Cutlashes." They ordered the captain, Andrew Crumpsty, and five of his crew to go on board the *Whydah*.[222] Learning that the *Mary Anne* was carrying a load of wine—more than seven thousand gallons of it—several of the pirates were sent on board to collect it. But they found that the heavy cable was coiled in the hatchway, making it impossible to get into the hold with so few hands. Undeterred, one of the pirates, Van Vorst, reportedly told one of the captives, Mackonochie, that if Mackonochie didn't help him get to the other wine on board, Van Vorst would "break his Neck." Fortunately for Mackonochie, the pirates found five bottles of fresh wine in the captain's cabin to tide them over. The pirates then told the prisoners aboard the *Mary Anne* that they had a commission from King George I and that they would "stretch it to the Worlds end." Bellamy ordered his men to bring the *Mary Anne* with them until they could find a good place to stop and plunder the rest of the wine.[223]

The two pirate vessels and their new prize then continued their way north, but by late afternoon, a very thick fog had rolled in, reducing visibility significantly. In this weather, Bellamy knew it would be incredibly dangerous to try to make for the shore at Cape Cod due to the numerous unmarked shoals surrounding the coast. Bellamy decided to sit tight and wait for the fog to pass, so all three vessels came to a stop not far from each other. After about half an hour of waiting, the pirates caught sight of a sloop, the *Fisher*, heading straight toward them. It was a merchant sloop captained by Robert Ingols, carrying tobacco and hides to Boston from Virginia. As the *Fisher* neared the *Whydah*, reports indicate that Bellamy called out to the men of the *Fisher*, asking "whether the Master was Acquainted here," to which Captain Ingols replied that "he knew it very well." Realizing the value that a man like Ingols held in that moment, the pirates ordered Captain Ingols and his first mate to come aboard the *Whydah* and sent 4 armed men of their own to the *Fisher* so they could sail the sloop behind the flagship. As it was growing dark, Bellamy ordered

THE

HISTORY

OF

THE PIRATES,

CONTAINING

THE LIVES

OF

THOSE NOTED PIRATE CAPTAINS,

MISSON, BOWEN, KIDD, TEW, HALSEY, WHITE, CONDENT,
BELLAMY, FLY, HOWARD, LEWIS, CORNELIUS,
WILLIAMS, BURGESS, NORTH,

AND THEIR SEVERAL CREWS.

ALSO,

AN ACCOUNT OF THE PIRACIES AND CRUELTIES

OF

JOHN AUGUR, WILLIAM CUNNINGHAM, DENNIS MACKARTHY,
WILLIAM DOWLING, WILLIAM LEWIS, THOMAS MORRIS,
GEORGE BENDALL, AND WILLIAM LING,

WHO WERE TRIED, CONDEMNED AND EXECUTED

AT NASSAU, NEW PROVIDENCE,

ON THE

TENTH OF DECEMBER, 1718.

TO WHICH IS ADDED,

A CORRECT ACCOUNT OF

THE LATE PIRACIES

COMMITTED IN THE WEST-INDIES;

AND THE

EXPEDITION OF COMMODORE PORTER.

———

Omne tulit punctum, qui miscuit utile dulci.—*Hor.*

———

HARTFORD :

PUBLISHED BY HENRY BENTON.

———

1834.

The frontispiece for the publication *The History of the Pirates Containing the Lives of Those Noted Pirate Captains Misson, Bowen, Kidd, Tew, Halsey, White, Condent, Bellamy...*, 1834. *Courtesy of the Library of Congress.*

each vessel to place a large lamp on their stern so the four ships could keep sight of each other as they headed north. Bellamy had about 130 men on the *Whydah* in addition to most of their recent prisoners. Trailing behind was the *Anne Galley* with roughly 18 pirates on board, the *Mary Anne* under the control of 8 of Bellamy's men and around 2 prisoners, and the *Fisher*, on which there were 4 pirates to guard the *Fisher*'s remaining crew.[224]

Bellamy then told Simon Van Vorst and the pirates sailing the *Mary Anne* to "make more haste," to which a very drunk John Brown replied that "he would carry Sail till she carryed her Masts away." Meanwhile, the pirates "Drank plentifully of the Wine on board," taking turns at the helm. By around ten o'clock that night, "the Weather grew so thick, it Lightned and Rained hard, and was so very dark" to the point that they could not see the shore until they were among the breakers. According to an eyewitness account, one of the pirates warned the captive, Mackonochie, who was at the helm at the time, that he would shoot Mackonochie through the head "as he would a Dog and he should never tell his story," believing Mackonochie steered them toward the breakers on purpose. Between ten and eleven o'clock, the *Mary Anne* ran aground just south of Cape Cod. The pirates, fearful of being apprehended by authorities, allegedly cried out, "For God's sake let us go down into the Hould & Die together!" The men all rode out the storm on the vessel, at one point asking one of their captives to "Read to them the Common-Prayer Book," which he did for about an hour. By daybreak, the men found they could make their way to a nearby island where the pirates ate "sweetmeats" and drank wine that had washed ashore from the *Mary Anne*. After several hours, they were rescued by John Cole and William Smith, who "came over to the Island in a Cannoe, and carry'd the Pinks Company to the Main Land." Upon arriving at the main shore, Mackonochie went directly to the authorities to relay his experience, at which point the pirates were apprehended in Eastham and brought to Boston to await trial on charges of piracy.[225]

It appears that the men aboard the *Anne Galley* and the *Fisher* were more fortunate (perhaps because they were less inebriated). As the storm moved in the night of April 26, the men of the *Fisher* lost sight of the *Whydah*'s light. But, still seeing the light aboard the *Anne Galley*, the two ships stuck close together. Somehow, the crew of the *Anne Galley* safely navigated to shore, the *Fisher* right behind them, and both ships anchored for the night to wait out the storm. The next morning, around ten o'clock, the two vessels cut their cables and headed eastward, stopping just three leagues from Cape Cod. There, the pirates took "what they pleased" and ordered the *Fisher*'s men to board the *Anne Galley* before cutting the *Fisher*'s "Mast off by the board," leaving the hatches of the sloop open and leaving it "afloat in the Sea." The men then made their way to Monhegan, a small island on the coast of Maine, off Pemaquid Point. Landing on April 29, "they stayed and waited for the aforesaid Ship *Wedaw* Some time, but she came not." Believing at that point that the *Whydah* was lost in the storm, the pirates fitted out their longboat and headed to Matinicus, a small island farther east, just south of Rockland. During that time, the pirates seized a sloop, a shallop, and three schooners, taking the sloop and shallop back to Monhegan. Although the pirates dismissed the schooners, they did take the sails and compasses out of them first. Placing ten of their own on board the new sloop, they attacked another sloop lying near Pemaquid. Meanwhile, two shallops from Marblehead had the misfortune of crossing paths with the *Mary Anne* at Monhegan. The pirates forced the shallops to anchor, holding their crews hostage until the prize sloop returned. Then, taking everything they thought fit from each ship and loading it all into the prize sloop, the pirates "left the Snow and all the rest behind." Leaving the prisoners "to [their] Libertyes," the pirates "ordered the Skipper of the Shallope to carry" all of the captives to Marblehead, where they arrived on May 10, 1717.[226]

BELLAMY GETS WRECKED

Given that there were only two survivors of the *Whydah* shipwreck, details as to its demise are lacking in comparison to the rest of their fleet. But we do know that the ship lay quite low in the water, weighed down by a vast array of commodities and treasure. The *Whydah* is believed to have been carrying "elephant tusks, sugar, molasses, rum, cloth, quinine bark, indigo, and a ton of dry goods…[as well as] precious metal, 180 sacks of coin, each sack weighing fifty pounds." And as the storm raged off the New England coast, Bellamy and the men of the *Whydah* found themselves alone among the waves. They couldn't see any of their consort as they desperately tried to steer away from the dangers of the coast. But the more they tried to turn course, the worse their situation became. At one point, the men found the ship's bow confronting the wind directly. According to Barry Clifford, Bellamy probably resorted to a desperate measure sailors called "club-hauling," which "was meant to turn the ship around" in order to "face the waves and avoid being capsized."[227] With the lines taut, the pirates probably realized that there was no escape, and it's quite probable that many of the men had already been thrown or washed overboard. According to one of the two survivors of the *Whydah*'s wreck, Thomas Davis, "they cut their Cables and ran a shoar," and within fifteen minutes of hitting a sandbar, the ship had begun to roll, the mainmast was shattered, and the ship's rigging was torn apart. By morning, the *Whydah* was "beat to pieces." Clifford surmises that those who had survived so far may have tried to make their way to shore, but in "water so cold, there were few who could make" the five-hundred-foot swim. Those that did "froze to death trying to climb the steep sand cliffs of Eastham."[228] Out of 146 men on board, over a dozen of them captives, including Captain Crumpstey, there were only 2 survivors. In all, 144 men lost their lives in the tempest.

Early the next morning, residents of the Cape Cod coast awoke to a gruesome sight. As the waves ebbed and flowed, "bloated, mangled corpses" slowly piled onto the shore. Reports from Cyprian Southack, a naval veteran and Massachusetts local, began arriving quickly. One on May 5, 1717, noted that at least fifty-four white men and four Africans had "Come a shore Ded" from the wreck. Another report on May 8 described how the coroner, Samuel Freeman, demanded payment of eighty-three pounds for the burial of seventy-two wreck victims. In his journal on May 9, Southack reported seventy-six had, to date, come "on shoar out of the Pirate Ship dead."[229] In the meantime, the two *Whydah* survivors, Thomas Davis and John Julian (a Miskito Indian), were taken to the Boston jail to await trial.[230]

Mooncussers versus Cyprian Southack

Massachusetts Bay's governor, Samuel Shute, immediately set about trying to prevent locals from fishing the wreck so that his agents could recover the treasure without molestation. On April 30, 1717, Governor Shute authorized naval veteran Cyprian Southack "to seize what goods merchandise or Effects have or may be found or taken from the Piratts Ship Wreck att Cape Codd."[231] Although Southack tried to recover the *Whydah*'s lost treasure per Governor Shute's orders, his arrival at the wreck made his efforts too little too late. In one of his letters to Governor Shute, Southack informed the governor that his deputies, Mr. Little, Mr. Russell, and Mr. Cuttler, had ridden at least thirty miles up and down the shore near the wreck. According to his deputies, the inhabitants had already claimed considerable riches from the site, but the residents remained tight-lipped, refusing to own up to what they'd gathered. One of the first people to fish the wreck was a local man named Samuel Harding, who had saved Thomas Davis. The two went back to the wreck together, making multiple trips back and forth between the site and Harding's house, leading Southack to assume that Harding "Gott much Riches" in that time.[232]

He found that the local residents had cut the vessel to pieces, with "Two hundred men at Least Plundring of her," and that all he could recover were the *Whydah*'s cables and some of the ship's sails to the value of £200. Some residents told Southack that "they Gott Riches Out of the sand," but he had failed to find anything washed ashore himself. And, despite his best attempts, he was unable to recover much from residents who had fished the wreck. By royal instruction, issued to all governors of Massachusetts Bay between 1701 and 1728, "any goods, money, or other estate of pirates or piratically taken" were to be seized and secured and an inventory sent to the crown. The crown would then determine the method of disposal.[233] Any attempt by locals to sell goods they had taken from the wreck site or received from any surviving pirates would be considered illegal.

It seems, however, that the residents were unbothered by technicalities, going so far as to boldly *advertise* an auction of the "Goods saved out of the Ship Whido Capt. Samuel Bellame Commander, a reputed Pirate." According to an announcement in the *Boston News-Letter*, the public auction would take place at Crown Coffee-House on the Long Wharf in Boston on June 21, 1717. Anyone interested in the auction could view the goods at the "Treasurer's Ware-House" in the days prior.[234] A similar advertisement appeared in the *Boston News-Letter* on July 22 and 29, 1717, which suggests that this first auction may have been unsuccessful. The July advertisement specified the sale of "two Anchors, two Great Guns, and some Junk, that came from the Wreck Whido," at "Publick Vendue by Mr. Ambrose Vincent at the Crown Coffee-house" on July 30.[235]

THE ENEMY OF MANKIND'S LONG AND SAD WALK TO THE TREE OF DEATH

After six long months languishing in prison, the seven survivors of the *Mary Anne* and one of the *Whydah* survivors were officially indicted for piracy. On October 18, 1717, a Justiciary Court of Admiralty was convened for seven

Richard Coote, First Earl of Bellomont, who led a vicious crusade against pirates in North America while serving as governor of New York, Massachusetts, and New Hampshire between 1697 and 1701, engraving by Samuel Smith Kilburn, circa 1777. *Courtesy of the New York Public Library.*

of the men in Boston, and the trial lasted until October 30. John Julian was the only person not to stand trial. Being a Miskito Indian, it is most likely that he faced his own horrible punishment, being sold into slavery in North America. According to author Colin Woodard, it's possible that John Julian was the "Julian the Indian" who was sold to John Quincy of Braintree, grandfather of Abigail Adams and great-grandfather of future president John Quincy Adams.[236] Simon Van Vorst, John Brown, Thomas Baker, Hendrick Quintor, Peter Cornelius Hoof, John Shuan, Thomas South, and Thomas Davis each stood accused of "Piracy, Robbery and Felony." After the charges were read, testimonies given, and a bunch of purposefully convoluted legal maneuvers executed, the attorney general, Mr. Dudley, "in a very handsome and learned Speech summed up the Evidence, and made his Remarks upon the whole." Then the prosecutor, Mr. Smith, observed to the court that even if the accused were truly "forced out of the respective Ships and Vessels, they belonged to, by Bellamy and Labous," that did not "excuse their Guilt, Since no case of Necessity can justify a direct violation of the Divine and Moral Law, and give one the liberty of Sinning."[237]

Smith went further, asking the court, if "one or two Ruffians having no Arms meet a Man in the High-way, and instead of threatnings and force, give him good Words" while they "put their hands in his Pockets and rob him of his Money, Are they not to be accounted Robbers because they did not draw a Sword or Pistol?" The prosecutor concluded his statement by humbly moving "His Excellency and the Honourable the Commissioners to proceed to pass Sentence of Death upon all and each of them, they being all equally Guilty." Afterward, the court cleared for consideration of the "Evidences and Pleadings." Ultimately, they declared Simon Van Vorst, John Brown, Thomas Baker, Hendrick Quintor, Peter Cornelius Hoof, and John Shuan guilty according to the indictment. Based on the evidence presented, the court found Thomas Smith and Thomas Davis each not guilty, and they were released. For the unfortunate six men found guilty of piracy, they were ordered to "be carried to the Place of Execution," where they would each "be hanged up by the Neck until…Dead." The court also decreed that each of the guilty men's "Lands, Tenements, Goods and Chattles be forfeited to the King, and brought into His Majesty's use."[238]

On November 15, 1717, as throngs of New Englanders stared at "the Miserables now standing on the Scaffold…[who] as the Last Minute came on, several of the Malefactors, discovered a great Consternation." While Baker and Hoof "appeared very distinguishingly" penitent, Brown on the other hand "behaved himself at such a rate, as one would hardly imagine that any *Compos Mentis*, could have done so."[239] According to the famous New England minister Cotton Mather, "In such amazing Terms did [Brown] make his Exit! With such Madness, [did he] Go to the Dead!"[240] And so it was that Death added six more to the tally of men who died as a result of Black Sam Bellamy's unbounded ambition.

PART V

THE LIFE OF THE DEAD IS PLACED IN THE MEMORY OF THE LIVING

Chapter 9

DEATH IS JUST ANOTHER PATH

The Legacy of Black Sam Bellamy and the End of Golden Age Pirates

Every person has a legacy. You may not know what your impact is, and it may not be something that you can write on your tombstone, but every person has an impact on this world.
—Dara Horn [241]

S o many legends, rumors, and unique interpretations of the events surrounding Bellamy's demise emerged in the days, years, and centuries after his death. Famous New England preacher Cotton Mather couldn't resist using the wreck of the *Whydah* to promote his gospel. In his sermon "Instructions to the Living, from the Condition of the Dead," Mather remarked on the compassion God had for New England in raining justice upon this "horrid crew of PIRATES" who visited their coast toward the end of April 1717. After "many other Depredations…A Storm was now raised and raging," at which point, according to Mather's version of events, the "Barbarous Wretches" decided they must save themselves and thus "horribly Murdered all their Prisoners…lest they should appear as Witnesses against them." Mather lamented, "Alas! How far the Wickedness of Men may carry them!"[242]

Mather then went on to describe parts of conversations ministers had with the prisoners on November 15, 1717, as they walked to the execution dock. When a minister asked Thomas Baker, "How do you find your Heart now disposed?" Baker replied that he realized that he was "guilty of all the

Sins in the World." But if Baker sought words of comfort, they were little, with the minister telling Baker that he knew Baker was "in a very Great Agony" but that the gates of Heaven "must be entered with such an Agony." Simon Van Vorst didn't fare much better. After Van Vorst allegedly confessed to be a "very Great Sinner," the minister asked him which sins weighed most heavily upon him, to which he replied, "My undutifulness unto my Parents; and my Profanation of the Sabbath." That wasn't quite the answer the minister wanted to hear, lambasting Van Vorst and his "miserable companions" for not being more forthcoming. According to the minister, the real crime for which they were being "chased from among the Living" was not just any sin but the sin of "Robbery, and Piracy!" The

A portrait of the famous Puritan minister Cotton Mather, active in the early eighteenth century, engraving by Peter Pelham, 1728. *Courtesy of the Metropolitan Museum of Art.*

minister further confronted Van Vorst with the fact that every nation had agreed that pirates were "Common Enemies of Mankind" and that they would "Extirpate them [the pirates] out of the World." In addition to the many miseries the pirates brought on people, they were also murderers. When Van Vorst attempted to once again claim to be a "forced man," the minister replied, "There is no man who can say, He is Forced unto any sin against the Glorious GOD. Forced! No; You had better have suffered any thing, than to have sinn'd as you have done. Better have died a Martyr by the cruel Hands of your Brethren than have become one of their Brethren."[243]

When it was John Brown's turn, he admitted to being a "most Miserable" sinner whose heart was "Wonderfully hardened." But the minister didn't believe a word that came out of Brown's mouth, telling Brown that his prayers and Bible reading were "rather for an Amusement, than from any real and lively Sentiment raised in you." The minister also remarked that God had "distinguished [Brown] from your Drowned Brethren by giving you a space to [repent], which was denied unto them," and that he was sorry Brown had "made no Better use of it." Peter Cornelius Hoof had a fairly short conversation with the minister as well, completing the conversation by noting, "My Death this Afternoon, 'tis nothing, 'tis nothing. 'Tis the wrath of a terrible GOD after Death abiding on me, which is all that I am afraid of." At the end of the sermon and his account of the lives and deaths of Bellamy's pirates, Mather forcefully declared this to be "the End of Piracy!"[244] Mather may have been a bit hasty in his declaration, but piracy was certainly in steep decline.

The Witch of Wellfleet

Bellamy's life may have ended that stormy day in April 1717, but what happened to his young lover? The legend goes that a few months after Bellamy's departure, Maria found herself in a most unwelcome, albeit not uncommon, predicament. She was young, unwed, and pregnant with Bellamy's child. She had few options. Had Bellamy still been in Eastham, the two could have wed before anyone became the wiser about her pregnancy. But he was long gone on his treasure-seeking venture. Another option was to marry a local boy before she began to show. Then everyone would believe the child was his, and all would be well. But folklore says that Maria "sought the dunes daily in anticipation of Bellamy's return." Bellamy had, after all, made her a promise. How could she turn around and give herself to another, even if to save herself what would surely be a terrible punishment in Puritan-run Eastham? According to the Massachusetts Act of 1692, those found guilty of "fornication" were to be fined and publicly whipped. Where could she turn?[245]

Her only option at that point was to confide in her parents. The legend says that her parents ordered her to reveal the name of the father, and when she refused, they banished her. Other versions say that the locals discovered her secret, and they were the ones who banished her, while still others say that Maria actually hid the pregnancy the whole time and went into self-exile. Regardless, each version results in the same outcome: Maria hid among the dunes to experience her pregnancy in peace. And thus, rumors began that Maria was a witch. When she was on the verge of giving birth, Maria made her way to her parents' barn to deliver the baby. According to legend, that night her father awoke to "inhuman cries of pain and terror," and following the screams, he found Maria in the barn cradling a dead child in her arms. Mr. Hallett immediately ran to get a doctor and a priest, but upon his return, "Maria's anguish had given way to calm." Allegedly, her father "watched as his once innocent and beautiful child transformed before his very eyes" as she "invoked Satan himself and cursed Bellamy," screaming that he "would pay for the death of her child."[246]

In another version, Maria was able to give birth in secret and the child lived for a short time. She allegedly hid the child in her uncle's barn, returning daily to feed them. In one version, while Maria was away, the child supposedly died of asphyxiation after inhaling a piece of straw. Her uncle found the dead child before she returned and hid in the barn to confront her. In another version, the child froze to death and Maria's uncle caught her burying the child on their farm. Maria was now suspected of murdering her child and was allegedly taken to the Eastham jail. Ultimately, after years in and out of jail, Maria was never made to stand trial. Some say she was released and allowed to return to her hut in the dunes. Legends about the death of the Witch of Wellfleet are as numerous as those about her life, but in the end, she died as a lonely, heartbroken social pariah.[247]

BELLAMY, MARIA, AND AESOP'S TABLES

Three grueling years after he told Walter Cronkite that he'd find the *Whydah*, Barry Clifford did just that. On July 20, 1984, he and his crew found three cannons, a cannonball, and a Spanish piece of eight marked "1688" from wreckage they believed to be the *Whydah*. After years of ups, downs, and uncertainty, the shipwreck was ultimately authenticated as being the *Whydah*, making it the first—and so far only—authenticated pirate shipwreck to be discovered. Finding the *Whydah* was just another beginning in Bellamy's legacy. In 2021, underwater archaeologists from the Whydah Pirate Museum discovered the skeletal remains of at least six of the pirates who were killed in the 1717 wreck. After extracting the remains from concretions, experts hope that using today's cutting-edge DNA technology might help the team restore the skeletal remains to any potential descendants or return them to their homelands for burial or interment. But archaeological remains weren't the only discoveries Clifford and his team made. One night in July 1998, before they were to take a crew from *National Geographic* to the wreck site, the team had dinner at a restaurant in Wellfleet named Aesop's Tables. Clifford described the restaurant, located in a colonial-era building, as a "sprawling, sagging structure with a sloping front yard, a candlelit dining room, and a steep, narrow staircase leading to a bar in the attic." According to the manager of the restaurant, after Clifford and his team left, "a man who was eating dinner alone at the far end of the bar went into the restroom." When he came out a short time later, the manager said he was "white and shaking, 'wearing the pallor of death.'" He told the manager, "I need to get out of here right away," handing a server his credit card "with trembling hands." When the server asked the gentleman what was wrong, he said, "You might think I'm going crazy here, but I just saw a ghost in your bathroom," describing the apparition as a "lovely young woman with flaxen hair." After the man signed his check, the server told the manager about the incident. The man who saw the ghostly gal? His name was Bellamy. According to Clifford, "I have no idea why this happened or what it means, if anything. I just know that it took place and needs to be reported here, because it seemed to be beyond coincidence."[248] Today, the search for more answers and artifacts from the *Whydah* continues.

Bellamy's life may have ended on April 26, 1717, lost to Davy Jones's Locker, but his story is far from over. For those of us who have dedicated our scholarly lives to studying the golden age pirates, whose names are often lost to us, Bellamy is something of an enigma. We know just enough about him to frame a narrative of his life and daring exploits but not enough to do his story justice. Perhaps Clifford said it best: we may not find all the missing pages, but "those pages and the clues to what are on them can be found beneath the cobalt blue of the Cape's sandy shore." And, like Clifford, "I will go back again and again, in hope that I can find them all."[249]

GLOSSARY

barque/bark—a vessel up to seventy feet long with one to three masts, each rigged with a single lug-sail

boatswain—the ship's officer in charge of sails, rigging, anchors, cables, etc.

brigantine—a two-masted vessel with the mainmast rigged with a fore-and-aft triangular sail and a fore- or mizzen-mast rigged with two square sails

careen—a way of cleaning and repairing the hull of a vessel by bringing it into a shallow, secluded, and tree-lined cove that has a mud or soft sand bottom

consort—a partner; often used to denote a party to an operations agreement between two or more privateer/pirate ships

cutlass—a heavy curved sword with a relatively short blade used primarily at sea

foremast (man)—the mast closest to the bow in vessels with more than one mast; a common sailor

frigate—a sailing warship of a size and armament just below that of a ship of the line

galley—includes any variation within a generic category of vessels that carried more than one mast and that could be rowed as well as sailed

guns—naval cannons, typically defined by their pound rating

hogshead—refers to a large barrel or cask holding sixty-three gallons

indigo—a type of plant (Indigo anil) that produces a blue dye

Jesuit's bark—bark from the chinchona tree that contains quinine, a remedy used for malaria and other fevers

ketch—a small vessel with two square-rigged masts

league—approximately three nautical miles

leeward—the direction opposite to that of the wind

livre—a unit of French silver currency worth about a sixth of a piece of eight during the early eighteenth century

logwood—a brownish-red dye prepared from the heartwood of *Haematoxylon campechianum*; often combined with an iron salt to produce a rich black dye

nautical mile—a unit used in measuring distances at sea, equal to approximately 2,025 yards (1,852 meters)

periagua—also known as *peraguas*, *perlagas*, *pirogues*, and *peregos*; a very large type of canoe, usually undecked and flat-bottomed, that was used in coastal waters, particularly off Cuba and Central America

pilot—a coastal navigator qualified to conduct a vessel to and from a port or through a particular region

pink—an early eighteenth-century term for a slow-sailing, bulk cargo hauler with a relatively broad, deep, and bulging hull and a narrow "pinked-off" stern; could be sailed by a very small crew

powder monkey—a young boy tasked with ferrying gunpowder from the powder magazine in the ship's hold to the artillery pieces

prize—an enemy ship captured at sea

quartermaster—the most important officer aboard an eighteenth-century pirate vessel

schooner—a vessel rigged with fore-and-aft sails on two or more masts and with a square topsail on the foremast

shallop—a large, heavy, undecked boat with a single fore-and-aft rigged mast

share—privateers and pirates of the seventeenth and eighteenth centuries operated on the principle of "no prey, no pay," and their crews received compensation in the form of a proportion of the value of captured prizes

sloop—a decked vessel with a single mast that was fore-and-aft rigged; sometimes an additional square-rigged topsail was added

snow—a two-masted square-rigger that carried a trysail on a pole mounted immediately aft of the mainmast

Spanish Main—this term was applied generally to the north coast of the mainland of South America, from Rio de la Hacha in the west to the border with the French colony of Cayenne in the east, during the early eighteenth century

strike (to)—the act of lowering the colors of a ship in token of surrender

ton—twenty quintals = twenty hundred weight = 2,440 avoirdupois = forty-two cubic feet

tonnage—the cargo capacity of a sailing ship in terms of volume; in 1694, the formula formally adopted in England was length of the vessel in feet, multiplied by its maximum beam in feet, multiplied by the depth of its hold below the main deck in feet, with the product divided by ninety-four

vendue—a sheriff's sale of goods for the purpose of satisfying a judgment given in a law court

victuals—provisions

windward—the direction from which the wind is coming

Windward Passage—the channel between the islands of Cuba and Hispaniola

Note: These glossary terms and definitions were found in Kinkor's The Whydah Sourcebook *(2003).*

NOTES

Prologue

1. From his 1783 pamphlet *Observations on the Commerce of the American States*, quoted in Johnson et al., *History of Domestic and Foreign Commerce*, 37.
2. Rediker, *Villains of All Nations*, 30.

Part I

3. Pavese, *This Business of Living*, 101.
4. "America and West Indies: July 1717, 1–15: 629. Peter Heywood, C. in C. of Jamaica, to the Council of Trade and Plantations, 3 July," in *Calendar of State Papers Colonial, America and West Indies*, vol. 29, *1716–17*, 336–44.
5. Clifford and Perry, *Expedition Whydah*, 24.
6. "3.3 Bellamy Genealogy," in Kinkor, "Whydah Sourcebook," 359; Felt, Massachusetts Archives Collection: Military, 1712–1747, 173–74.
7. "Deposition of Abijah Savage, Commander of the Sloop <u>Bonetta</u> of Antigua before His Excellency Walter Hamilton, Antigua. November 30, 1716," CO 137/11 no.45iii, in Kinkor, "Whydah Sourcebook," 83.
8. Historically, "West Country" has referred to a loosely defined area in the southwest of England. The area is typically understood to include all or parts of the counties of Devon (or Devonshire), Cornwall, Somerset, Dorset, and Bristol.

9. "Rhode Island Dispatch of May 3, 1717," *Boston News-Letter*, May 6, 1717, in Kinkor, "Whydah Sourcebook," 110.

10. "Information of Andrew Turbett, Master; and Robert Gilmore, Supercargo, of the ship Agnes of Glasgow before Lt. Governor Spotswood, Virginia. April 17, 1717," CO 5/1318 no.16ii, in Kinkor, "Whydah Sourcebook," 98.

11. "3.3.3.1 The Hittisleigh/Drewsteignton Bellamy Family," in Kinkor, "Whydah Sourcebook," 363.

12. Woodard, *Republic of Pirates*, 29–30.

13. Clark, "Farm Wages and Living Standards in the Industrial Revolution," 485.

14. Hanna, *Pirate Nests*, 24.

15. Quoted in Hanna, *Pirate Nests*, 49.

16. Ibid., 52.

17. Ibid., 40–43.

18. Ibid., 51.

19. Impressment, often referred to as press gangs, is a form of forced recruitment in which men were compelled into military or naval service with or without notice.

20. Selinger, *Pirates of New England*, 116–17; Clifford and Perry, *Expedition Whydah*, 72.

21. Konstam, *History of Pirates*, 96.

22. St. Clair, *Criminal Calendar*, preface.

23. Hawkins, *Observations of Sir Richard Hawkins*, 221–22.

24. Literally translated as "good war," in this context the phrase refers to viewing the three-day battle as part of a "good" or "legitimate" war, thus making Hawkins and his men prisoners of war subject to different laws than pirates. At this time, England and Spain had been unofficially at war since 1585, referred to as the Anglo-Spanish War (1585–1604).

25. "Richard Hawkins to the Earl of Essex, 14 November 1598," in *Calendar of the Manuscripts of the Most Hon. the Marquis of Salisbury*, 438.

26. "Richard Hawkins to Queen Elizabeth, 12 June 1598," in *Calendar of the Manuscripts of the Most Hon. the Marquis of Salisbury*, 209.

27. "Richard Hawkins to the Earl of Essex, 14 November 1598," in *Calendar of the Manuscripts of the Most Hon. the Marquis of Salisbury*, 439.

28. James I was the son of Mary Stuart (also known as Mary, Queen of Scots), Queen Elizabeth I's first cousin once removed. Since 1567, he had been serving as King James VI of Scotland. His ascension to the English throne in 1603 became known as the Union of the Crowns. Although

James ruled as monarch over England and Scotland, the two kingdoms remained sovereign states with their own parliaments, judiciaries, and laws until the Acts of Union in 1707, at which time they merged to form the Kingdom of Great Britain.

29. "Venice: October 1603: 141. Giovanni Carlo Scaramelli, Venetian Secretary in England, to the Doge and Senate, 5 October," in *Calendar of State Papers Relating to English Affairs in the Archives of Venice*, 99–109.

30. Surety is defined as when a person agrees to take responsibility for the actions of another, typically in the form of a financial guarantee. "Venice: October 1603: 146. A Proclamation to repress all Piracies and Depredations upon the Sea, Enclosure in 22 October dispatch," in *Calendar of State Papers Relating to English Affairs in the Archives of Venice*, 99–109.

31. James I, King of England, *By the King*.

32. Hanna, *Pirate Nests*, 55.

33. "Cecil Papers: January 1608, 1–15: Petition of Guillaume Bouillon to the King of France and his Council, 9 January 1607," in *Calendar of the Cecil Papers in Hatfield House: Volume 20*, 1–20.

34. "Cecil Papers: January 1608, 1–15: Statement of French vessels which have been taken and carried off by pirates in the ports and harbours of England…," in *Calendar of the Cecil Papers in Hatfield House: Volume 20*.

35. Hanna, *Pirate Nests*, 55–56.

36. Quoted in Hanna, *Pirate Nests*, 57.

37. Ibid., 63–64.

38. Smith, *True Travels, Adventures, and Observations*, ch. XXVIII.

39. Quoted in Hanna, *Pirate Nests*, 68.

40. Ibid., 69.

41. In other words, the letter's author commends acts of piracy against the Spanish because Spaniards are "limbs of the antichrist." Kingsbury, *Records of the Virginia Company of London*, 367; Hanna, *Pirate Nests*, 69.

42. Dow and Edmonds, *Pirates of the New England*, 2.

43. The English Civil War was technically three separate civil wars, each of which was fought between Royalists and Parliamentarians over how England should be governed and issues related to religious freedom. The First English Civil War occurred between 1642 and 1646 between King Charles I and the Long Parliament, which ended with Charles I being imprisoned. The Second Civil War began in 1648 when Charles I negotiated a secret treaty with the Scots. The Scots agreed to invade England and help restore Charles I to the throne, and in return, Charles

I promised to implement church reforms. Ultimately, the Royalists and Scots were defeated in August 1649 at the Battle of Preston, ending this second war. The Third Civil War, which occurred between 1649 and 1651, erupted when the Rump Parliament found King Charles I guilty of high treason and executed him on January 30, 1649. On one side of the conflict were those who supported the ascension of Charles, Prince of Wales (Charles I's eldest son), to the throne. On the other side were those who defended the Rump Parliament. After the Royalists were defeated at the Battle of Worcester on September 3, 1651, the Prince of Wales feared he would suffer the same fate as his father and escaped. He managed to reach France on October 16, 1651, and he lived there in exile until the Restoration in 1660.

44. "October 1650: An Act for prohibiting Trade with the Barbadoes, Virginia, Bermuda and Antego…, 3 October 1650," in *Acts and Ordinances of the Interregnum*, 425–29.

Part II

45. Capital crimes are those considered punishable by death. Although laws could vary widely between the colonies, there seemed to be a general consensus that committing crimes like sodomy, blasphemy, adultery, treason, and assault warranted execution. Some colonies were more uncompromising than others. In Virginia, Lieutenant Governor Sir Thomas Gates issued a strict list of criminal punishments in 1610, which contained at least forty-eight capital crimes. They ranged from picking flowers from the private garden of a neighbor to trading with local Indigenous people. But property crimes appear to be entirely absent from the Massachusetts Body of Liberties, published in 1641.

46. Bull's name also shows up in records as "Dixey" and "Dixy."

47. "America and West Indies: March 1632: Minute as above. Two patents to Sir Ferd. Gorges, Lieut. Col. Walter Norton, and their associates, 2 March 1632," in *Calendar of State Papers Colonial, America and West Indies*, vol. 1, 141–43.

48. Dow and Edmonds, *Pirates of the New England Coast*, 20; Winthrop, *Winthrop's Journal*, vol. I, 82.

49. Pemaquid is the site of what is presently Bristol, Maine.

50. Nye, "Pounds Sterling to Dollars."

51. Winthrop, *Winthrop's Journal*, vol. I, 95.

52. Dow and Edmonds, *Pirates of the New England Coast*, 21; Selinger, *Pirates of New England*, 30; Winthrop, *Winthrop's Journal*, vol. I, 95.
53. Gallup also appears in the records as "Gallopp" and "Gallop."
54. Winthrop, *Winthrop's Journal*, vol. I, 96.
55. Clap, *Memoirs of Capt. Roger Clap*, 19; Dow and Edmonds, *Pirates of the New England Coast*, 22; Winthrop, *Winthrop's Journal*, vol. I, 98, 102.
56. Clap, *Memoirs of Capt. Roger Clap*, 19.
57. Hanna, *Pirate Nests*, 89; Some may say that one (alleged) act of cannibalism does not a cannibal make. To that I ask: how many times does a person need to eat the flesh of their fellow humans before you can consider them a cannibal?
58. Winthrop, *Winthrop's Journal*, vol. I, 102.
59. Ibid., 108; Clap, *Memoirs of Capt. Roger Clap*, 19.
60. Also spelled as "Aquamenticus" or "Agamenticus," the site today is York, Maine.
61. Wampum, a traditional shell bead of the Eastern Woodlands tribes of North America, was often used as a form of currency in trade. It was New England's first legal form of currency and was widely used until the nineteenth century.
62. Underhill, *Nevves from America*, 10; Cave, "Who Killed John Stone?," 512–13; Winthrop, *Winthrop's Journal*, vol. I, 118.
63. Underhill, *Nevves from America*, 10.
64. The Western Niantic were a small, quasi-independent band of Natives who paid tribute to the Pequot. In turn, the Pequot provided the Western Niantic with protection.
65. Winthrop, *Winthrop's Journals*, vol. I, 139; Cave, "Who Killed John Stone?," 515.
66. Clap, *Memoirs of Capt. Roger Clap*, 20.
67. The island was actually first documented by a Basque explorer named Lope de Olano on November 25, 1510, but remained largely uninhabited until the English arrived in 1628, save for some Dutch and French pirates.
68. Winthrop, *Winthrop's Journal*, vol. I, 310.
69. These crises were the result of the crown not only barring the exportation of its sterling coins but also prohibiting the colonies from minting their own coins. This left each colony creating its own conventions and coin ratings. For example, the standard units in England were pounds (£), shillings (s.), and pence (d.) where £1 was the equivalent of 20s. and 1s. was the equivalent of 12d. But in many of the colonies, they created their own values for each unit, and those values were not standard across colonies.

New York money was not equal to Massachusetts money, which was not equal to South Carolina money, none of which was as valuable as sterling. Colonists also assigned their local currency values to foreign currency, like Spanish pieces of eight. For a detailed review of colonial currency, see McCusker, "British Colonial Exchange on London," 116–233.

70. Winthrop, *Winthrop's Journal: History of New England*, vol. II, 17.

71. Hanna, *Pirate Nests*, 91.

72. "July 1642: Ordinance for the Earl of Warwick to remain in his Command of the Fleet, 1 July 1642," in *Acts and Ordinances of the Interregnum*, 12.

73. Maracaibo is located in present-day Venezuela. Trujillo (also referenced in sources as Truxillo) is located in present-day Peru.

74. Hanna, *Pirate Nests*, 90–92.

75. "Lustie" is an obsolete spelling of the term "lusty," referring to someone who is eager, energetic, spirited, or full of vigor.

76. Bradford, *Bradford's History "Of Plimoth Plantation,"* 269; Winthrop, *Winthrop's Journal*, vol. II, 272.

77. Sedan chairs were all the rage in the seventeenth century since streets were generally filled with mud, garbage, and excrement, which was not only a health hazard but also simply unpleasant to walk through. Although they were little more than a seat inside a cabin mounted on two poles, sedan chairs were popular with the gentry because it enabled them to "keep up appearances." In this case, it kept their shoes clean. Sedan chairs also typically featured a detachable roof, allowing upper-class women to wear the tall, elaborate headdresses that were fashionable at the time. The sedan chair was carried by two men called "chairmen," one at the front and one at the rear.

78. Bradford, *Bradford's History "Of Plimoth Plantation,"* 269; Winthrop, *Winthrop's Journal*, vol. II, 272.

79. Winthrop, *Winthrop's Journal*, vol. II, 273; Bradford, *Bradford's History "Of Plimoth Plantation,"* 269.

80. Bradford, *Bradford's History "Of Plimoth Plantation,"* 269; Hanna, *Pirate Nests*, 93.

81. "America and West Indies: December 1646: 9. Robt. Earl of Warwick to Adam Winthrop, David Yale, Ant. Stoddard, and Benj. Gillam, merchants at Boston, 11 December 1646," in *Calendar of State Papers Colonial, America and West Indies*, vol. 1, 327; Hanna, *Pirate Nests*, 93.

82. Heather Brooke, "Royal Appetite for Secrecy Can Only Invite Scandal," *The Guardian*, May 24, 2010, www.theguardian.com/commentisfree/libertycentral/2010/may/24/royal-appetite-secrecy-only-invite-scandal.

83. Selinger, *Pirates of New England*, 25.

84. Hutchinson, *History of the Colony of Massachuset's Bay*, 177.

85. Bullion refers to highly pure physical gold and silver, which is often kept in the form of bars, ingots, or coins. Not to be confused with *bouillon*, another word for "broth," which is a delicious and savory liquid typically used as a base for dishes like soups, sauces, and gravies. It even comes in a dehydrated form called bouillon cubes (although I don't recommend trying to use it as a form of currency!).

86. Hutchinson, *History of the Colony of Massachuset's Bay*, 177–78; Hanna, *Pirate Nests*, 98–99.

87. Dow, *Records and Files of the Quarterly Courts of Essex County, Massachusetts*, 314–18.

88. Hanna, *Pirate Nests*, 99.

89. Dolin, *Black Flags, Blue Waters*, 16; Hanna, *Pirate Nests*, 99.

90. Quoted in Hanna, *Pirate Nests*, 101.

91. Ibid., 101.

92. Hispaniola is a Caribbean Island in the Greater Antilles. Today, it is home to Haiti and the Dominican Republic.

93. Dolin, *Black Flags, Blue Waters*, 22–23; Hanna, *Pirate Nests*, 102.

94. Hanna, *Pirate Nests*, 107.

95. Ibid., 144.

96. B–, "Letter to a Member of Parliament Concerning the Suppression of Piracy"; Hanna, *Pirate Nests*, 145–46.

97. "America and West Indies: February 1684: 1563. Sir Thomas Lynch to Lords of Trade and Plantations, 28 February 1684," in *Calendar of State Papers Colonial, America and West Indies*, vol. 11, 581–601; Dolin, *Black Flags, Blue Waters*, 31, 38; B–, "Letter to a Member of Parliament Concerning the Suppression of Piracy."

98. Ogg, *England in the Reign of Charles II*, 344–46; Hutton, "Making of the Secret Treaty of Dover," 308.

99. *Recusant* was a term applied to those who remained loyal to the Catholic Church, refusing to attend services in the Church of England after the English Reformation; Ogg, *England in the Reign of Charles II*, 346–48; Harris, *Restoration*, 71.

100. Boxer, "Some Second Thoughts on the Third Anglo-Dutch War," 70–74; Clodfelter, *Warfare and Armed Conflicts*, 46.

101. New York had previously been a Dutch colony called New Netherland until the English captured it in 1664. The English renamed the area in honor of James, Duke of York, the brother of King Charles II.

102. At that time, the Netherlands was known as the Republic of the Seven United Netherlands. Quoted in Dow and Edmonds, *Pirates of the New England Coast*, 44.

103. Dow and Edmonds, *Pirates of the New England Coast*, 44; Selinger, *Pirates of New England*, 34.

104. Pentagoet is located in present-day Castine, Maine.

105. Dow and Edmonds, *Pirates of the New England Coast*, 44.

106. The Bay of Fundy is situated between New Brunswick and Nova Scotia.

107. Dow and Edmonds, *Pirates of the New England Coast*, 45; Selinger, *Pirates of New England*, 34–35.

108. Dow and Edmonds, *Pirates of the New England Coast*, 45; Selinger, *Pirates of New England*, 35–36.

109. Dow and Edmonds, *Pirates of the New England Coast*, 46–47; Selinger, *Pirates of New England*, 36–37.

110. Dow and Edmonds, *Pirates of the New England Coast*, 48–52; Selinger, *Pirates of New England*, 37–39; "America and West Indies: October 1676: 1071. Answer of the Governor and Council of Massachusetts to the complaint of the Extraordinary Ambassador of the StatesGeneral…, 18 October 1676," in *Calendar of State Papers Colonial, America and West Indies*, vol. 9, 459–81.

111. "Charles II, 1660: An Act for the Encourageing and increasing of Shipping and Navigation.," in *Statutes of the Realm*, vol. 5, 246–50.

112. "Charles II, 1663: An Act for the Encouragement of Trade," in *Statutes of the Realm*, vol. 5, 449–52.

113. "America and West Indies: September 1675: 662. Gov. Leverett to the Lord Privy Seal [Earl of Anglesey], 6 September 1675," in *Calendar of State Papers Colonial, America and West Indies*, vol. 9, 271–93.

114. "America and West Indies: September 1675: 673. Governor Lord Vaughan to Sec. Sir Joseph Williamson, 20 September 1675," in *Calendar of State Papers Colonial, America and West Indies*, vol. 9.

115. "America and West Indies: February 1676: 813. Journal of the Lords of Trade and Plantations, 4 February 1676," in *Calendar of State Papers Colonial, America and West Indies*, 345–55.

116. "America and West Indies: March 1676: 849. Inquiries given to Edward Randolph, 20 March 1676," in *Calendar of State Papers Colonial, America and West Indies*, vol. 9, 355–65.

117. "America and West Indies: March 1676: 838. The King to the Governor and Magistrates 'of our town of Boston in New England,' 10 March 1676," in *Calendar of State Papers Colonial, America and West Indies*, vol. 9, 355–65.

118. Despite his damning observations, Randolph praises Plymouth and Connecticut, where the "laws of England are observed, the oath of allegiance taken…the Navigation Acts are observed…[and] the people are loyal." "America and West Indies: October 1676: 1067. Answer of Edward Randolph to several heads of inquiry concerning the present state of New England, 12 October 1676," in *Calendar of State Papers Colonial, America and West Indies*, vol. 9, 459–81.

119. Washburn, *Sketches of the Judicial History of Massachusetts*, 91.

120. "America and West Indies: May 1–15, 1677: 218. Representation of Edward Randolph, 6 May 1677," in *Calendar of State Papers Colonial, America and West Indies*, vol. 10, 72–88.

121. Crowell and Choate, "Trial and Punishment of Mr. Wise and His Fellow-Citizens, August 1687," in *History of the Town of Essex*, 102.

122. "America and West Indies: September 1684: 1862. II Relation of T. Thacker, Deputy-Collector, 16 August 1684," in *Calendar of State Papers Colonial, America and West Indies*, vol. 11, 682–94.

123. "America and West Indies: October 1683, 1–15: 1299. Extract from a letter of Governor Cranfield, 7 October 1683," in *Calendar of State Papers Colonial, America and West Indies*, vol. 11, 511–18.

124. "America and West Indies: September 1684: 1862. William Dyre to Sir Leoline Jenkins, 12 August 1684," in *Calendar of State Papers Colonial, America and West Indies*, vol. 11, 682–94.

125. Quoted in Hanna, *Pirate Nests*, 180.

126. Hanna, *Pirate Nests*, 180.

127. Quoted in Hanna, *Pirate Nests*, 181.

Part III

128. Quoted in Hanna, *Pirate Nests*, 5.

129. Niles, "French on Block Island," 5–6.

130. "America and West Indies: July 1690: 994. Abstracts of several letters written to Thomas Brinley, from New England, 24 July 1690," in *Calendar of State Papers Colonial, America and West Indies*, vol. 13, 291–301; Dolin, *Black Flag, Blue Waters*, 38–39.

131. Niles, "French on Block Island," 8–9; Dolin, *Black Flags, Blue Waters*, 39.

132. "America and West Indies: May 1698, 26–31: 521. Edward Randolph to Council of Trade and Plantations, 30 May 1698," in *Calendar of State Papers Colonial, America and West Indies*, vol. 16, 244–59; Hanna, *Pirate Nests*, 215.

133. For a full transcript of the Act, see "William III, 1698–9: An Act for the more effectuall Suppressions of Piracy. [Chapter VII. Rot. Parl. 11 Gul. III. p. 2. n. 5.]," in *Statutes of the Realm*, vol. 7, 590–94.

134. Whitehead, "Letter to Mr. Basse About Pyrats & Piracies, 22 July 1696," in *Documents Relating to the Colonial History of the State of New Jersey*, 156.

135. Whitehead, "L[ette]r from Mr Jerem[iah] Bass ab[ou]t Pirates & Piracies, 26 July 1696," in *Documents Relating to the Colonial History of the State of New Jersey*, 157–59.

136. Hanna, *Pirate Nests*, 189.

137. Johnson, *History of the Pyrates*, vol. II, 85–86.

138. Known as the "gateway of anguish" or "gate of grief" due to the dangers the strait posed for navigators, it is located between Djibouti and Eritrea in the Horn of Africa and Yemen on the Arabian Peninsula, thereby connecting the Red Sea to the Gulf of Aden.

139. Johnson, *History of the Pyrates*, vol. II, 86–87.

140. "America and West Indies: May 1698, 16–20: 473. Governor the Earl of Bellomont to Council of Trade and Plantations," in *Calendar of State Papers Colonial, America and West Indies*, vol. 16, 217–34; "America and West Indies: January 1699, 1–14: 26. T. Weaver to the Council of Trade and Plantations," in *Calendar of State Papers Colonial, America and West Indies*, vol. 17, 1–19.

141. "America and West Indies: July 1698, 6–9: 647. Governor Goddard to the Duke of Shrewsbury," in *Calendar of State Papers Colonial, America and West Indies*, vol. 16, 322–28.

142. Hanna, *Pirate Nests*, 192–93.

143. Johnson, *History of the Pyrates…* vol. II, 108–9.

144. "America and West Indies: January 1697, 16–30: 604. Council of Trade and Plantations to Lieutenant-Governor Stoughton, 20 January 1697," in *Calendar of State Papers Colonial, America and West Indies*, vol. 15, 308–37.

145. Not to be confused with the pirate Edward Hull.

146. "America and West Indies: January 1697, 1–15: 554. Copy of a letter from Benjamin Davis of Boston to Edward Hull, merchant, of London, 2 January 1697," in *Calendar of State Papers Colonial, America and West Indies*, vol. 15, 289–308.

147. Smith, *True Travels, Adventures, and Observations*, ch. XXVIII.

148. Gardner, *Grendel*, 74.

149. Dolin, *Black Flags, Blue Waters*, 120; "America and West Indies: December 1701, 2–5: 1054. Geo. Larkin to the Council of Trade and Plantations, 5 December 1701," in *Calendar of State Papers Colonial, America and West Indies*, vol. 19, 630–59.

150. In the Acts of 1707, the separate kingdoms of England and Scotland united into a single Kingdom of Great Britain.

151. Placentia is a town located in present-day Newfoundland and Labrador, a province of Canada.

152. His ascension to the throne as King George I ended the Stuart Dynasty and gave rise to the Hanoverian Dynasty.

153. "America and West Indies: May 1705: 1105. C. Hobby to the Council of Trade and Plantations, 8 May 1705," in *Calendar of State Papers Colonial, America and West Indies*, vol. 22, 510–24.

154. Dudley, "Copy of Capt. Plowman's Commission," in *Arraignment, Tryal, and Condemnation of Capt. John Quelch*, 20; Dolin, *Black Flags, Blue Waters*, 123.

155. Dudley, "Copy of Capt. Plowman's Instructions," in *Arraignment, Tryal, and Condemnation of Capt. John Quelch*, 20–21; Dolin, *Black Flags, Blue Waters*, 123–24.

156. Dudley, "Copy of Capt. Daniel Plowman's Letters to Two of the Owners," in *Arraignment, Tryal, and Condemnation of Capt. John Quelch*, 22.

157. According to the court transcript from *Arraignment, Tryal, and Condemnation of Capt. John Quelch*, Plowman died on August 6, although it is unclear whether he was murdered or died from his illness; Ames et al., "Ch. 47, 1704–1705," in *Acts and Resolves*, vol. VIII, 387.

158. Dudley, "Copy of the Owners Letter sent to the severall Islands, in the West Indies, 18 August 1703," in *Arraignment, Tryal, and Condemnation of Capt. John Quelch*, 22–23.

159. Farine is a wheat flour but also refers to a type of animal feed. Dudley, *Arraignment, Tryal, and Condemnation of Capt. John Quelch*, 2–3.

160. Ibid., 3–4.

161. Ibid., 10–12.

162. Dolin, *Black Flags, Blue Waters*, 127–28.

163. Ames et al., "By the Honourable Thomas Povey, Esq. Lieut. Governor and Commander in Chief, for the time being, of Her Majesty's Province of the Massachusetts Bay in New-England: A Proclamation," in *Acts and Resolves*, 388.

164. Dolin, *Black Flags, Blue Waters*, 133, 136–37.

165. *Account of the Behaviour and Last Dying Speeches of the Six Pirates*; Dolin, *Black Flags, Blue Waters*, 138.

166. *Account of the Behaviour and Last Dying Speeches of the Six Pirates*; Dolin, *Black Flags, Blue Waters*, 140–41; Ames et al., "Extract from the Diary of Samuel Sewall, vol. II," in *Acts and Resolves*, 394.

167. "America and West Indies: July 1704, 11–20: 451. Humble Address of the Council and Assembly of the Massachusetts Bay to the Queen, 12 July 1704," in *Calendar of State Papers Colonial, America and West Indies*, vol. 22, 211–23.

168. "America and West Indies: May 1705: 1105. C. Hobby to the Council of Trade and Plantations, 8 May 1705," in *Calendar of State Papers Colonial, America and West Indies*, vol. 22.

169. Dolin, *Black Flags, Blue Waters*, 142–43.

170. Ames et al., *Acts and Resolves*, 397.

171. Beal, *Quelch's Gold*, 209.

172. Dolin, *Black Flags, Blue Waters*, 145–46.

173. Rediker, *Villains of All Nations*, 6, 19.

174. Ibid., 25–26.

Part IV

175. In a speech to Captain Beer according to Johnson, *History of the Pyrates*, vol. II, 204.

176. Eastham is located on the so-called forearm of Cape Cod.

177. Brunelle, *Bellamy's Bride*, 17–20.

178. Ibid., 24, 27.

179. The 1715 Spanish fleets wrecked off the east coast of Florida between present-day Vero Beach and Sebastian, Florida.

180. Williams also appears in the records as "Paul" and "Paulgrave."

181. Dolin, *Black Flags, Blue Waters*, 176–77; Selinger, *Pirates of New England*, 117.

182. Selinger, *Pirates of New England*, 117–18.

183. IYKYK (if you know, you know). Selinger, *Pirates of New England*, 118.

184. Initially, the term *periagua* or *piragua* was used to denote dugout canoes used by many Indigenous peoples in the Caribbean. By the 1700s, the term was being used to refer to a flat-bottomed boat with one or two masts that could also be rowed by the small crew it held.

185. His name has also appeared as "Cornelius" in several of the testimonies of Bellamy's surviving men.

186. He also appears in the records as "Peter Hove."

187. *Trials of eight persons indited for piracy*, 12.

188. The vessel also appears as *St. Mary* in several archival documents.

189. "Deposition of Allen Bernard, Jamaica, 10 August 1716," Jamaican Council Minutes, ff. 63–68 in Kinkor, "Whydah Sourcebook," 62–63.

190. "Memorial of Monsr. Moret," Jamaican Council Minutes, ff. 17–23, in Kinkor, "Whydah Sourcebook," 50.

191. Hornigold also appears in the records as "Hornygold," which honestly just seems appropriate. The ship *Marianne* also shows up in the records as *Mary Anne*. "M.le Comte de Blenac, [Governor of the French Settlements in Hispaniola] to Governor Lord A. Hamilton: Leogane, July 18th 1716," CO 137/12 no. 21ii, in Kinkor, "Whydah Sourcebook," 48.

192. "Deposition of Joseph Eels, Port Royal, Jamaica, 3 December 1716," CO 137/12 no. 411i, in Kinkor, "Whydah Sourcebook," 63–64.

193. "Deposition of Joseph Eels," in Kinkor, "Whydah Sourcebook," 64; Dolin, *Black Flags, Blue Waters*, 178.

194. The pirates of the Flying Gang saw New Providence as the perfect location for a "Pirate Republic." The island lacked any semblance of a legitimate government and was ideally situated in proximity to most of the major shipping routes.

195. "Examination of Jeremiah Higgins, New York, 22 June 1717," Records of the Vice-Admiralty Court of the Province of New York 1685–1838, in Kinkor, "Whydah Sourcebook," 161. There were many variations of La Buse: "La Bouche," "Labous," "La Boos," and "La Buze," to name a few.

196. How willing Quintor was to join the pirates is debatable. See "[The Substance of The] Examination of Hendrick Quintor, Boston, 6 May 1717," in Kinkor, "Whydah Sourcebook," 125.

197. "The Substance of the Examinations of John Brown, &c. Taken by Order of His Excellency the GOVERNOUR, on Monday the 6th of May, 1717," in *Trials of eight persons indited for piracy*, 23; Dolin, *Black Flags, Blue Waters*, 180–81.

198. "Examination of Jeremiah Higgins," in Kinkor, "Whydah Sourcebook," 161–62; "Examination of Richard Caverley, New York, 15 June 1717," Records of the Vice-Admiralty Court of the Province of New York 1685–1838, in Kinkor, "Whydah Sourcebook," 157–58.

199. "Examination of Jeremiah Higgins," in Kinkor, "Whydah Sourcebook," 161–62; "Examination of Richard Caverley," in Kinkor, "Whydah Sourcebook," 157–58; Clifford and Perry, *Expedition Whydah*, 222.

200. "Deposition of Abijah Savage, Commander of the Sloop *Bonetta* of Antigua before His Excellency Walter Hamilton, Antigua, 30 November 1716," CO 137/11, no. 45iii, in Kinkor, "Whydah Sourcebook," 81–82.

201. Nye, "Pounds Sterling to Dollars."

202. Maugh, "Pirate's Life for Him."

203. "Deposition of Abijah Savage," 83.

204. "The Substance of the Examination of Simon Van Vorst," in *Trials of eight persons indited for piracy*, 25.

205. "Examination of Richard Caverley," in Kinkor, "Whydah Sourcebook," 158; Dolin, *Black Flags, Blue Waters*, 182.

206. Saba is an island that is part of the Leeward Islands, or the northern portion of the Lesser Antilles, located southeast of the Virgin Islands.

207. *Trials of eight persons indited for piracy*, 18–19.

208. In a speech to Captain Beer according to Johnson, *History of the Pyrates*, vol. II, 204.

209. "3.4 Lawrence Prince," in Kinkor, "Whydah Sourcebook," 365; Woodard, *Republic of Pirates*, 156–57; "The Substance of the Examinations of John Brown, &c.," in *Trials of eight persons indited for piracy*, 23.

210. Clifford and Perry, *Expedition Whydah*, 247; Woodard, *Republic of Pirates*, 157.

211. An island in the Bahamas, not to be confused with Long Island, New York.

212. *Trials of eight persons indited for piracy*, 25; Woodard, *Republic of Pirates*, 170.

213. *Trials of eight persons indited for piracy*, 23–25; Woodard, *Republic of Pirates*, 170.

214. Böhne and Simons, "Marteau Early 18th-Century Currency Converter."

215. "Rhode Island Dispatch of 3 May 1717," *Boston News-Letter*, May 6, 1717, in Kinkor, "Whydah Sourcebook," 110.

216. Johnson, *History of the Pyrates*, vol. II, 204.

217. Ibid., vol. II, 204.

218. "Examination of Richard Caverley," in Kinkor, "Whydah Sourcebook," 158.

219. In the deposition of Andrew Turbett and Robert Gilmore, they note that the *Endeavor* came from Brightelmstone, a former fishing village located in present-day Brighton. But in John Brown's testimony, he notes the ship was from Bristol.

220. "Information of Andrew Turbett, Master; and Robert Gilmore," in Kinkor, "Whydah Sourcebook," 98; "The Substance of the Examinations of John Brown, &c.," in *Trials of eight persons indited for piracy*, 23.

221. "Information of Andrew Turbett, Master; and Robert Gilmore," in Kinkor, "Whydah Sourcebook," 98–99; "Anonymous to Council of Trade and Plantations, Rappahannock, Virginia, 15 April 1717," CO 5/1318 no. 4, in Kinkor, "Whydah Sourcebook," 97.

222. The captain's name also appears as "Crumsty" and "Crumpsley."

223. "109. Deposition of Thomas FitzGerald and Alexander Mackonochie, 6 May 1717," in Jameson, *Privateering and Piracy in the Colonial Period*, 296; *Trials of eight persons indited for piracy*, 9–10; Clifford and Perry, *Expedition Whydah*, 258.

224. "109. Deposition of Thomas FitzGerald and Alexander Mackonochie, 6 May 1717," in Jameson, *Privateering and Piracy in the Colonial Period*, 296–97; "111. Deposition of Ralph Merry and Samuel Roberts, 11 and 16 May 1717," in *Privateering and Piracy in the Colonial Period*, 301; Woodard, *Republic of Pirates*, 181.

225. *Trials of eight persons indited for piracy*, 9–10; "Deposition of James Donovan, Boston, 6 May 1717, Jur. at 8 May 1717," Suffolk Court Files, MA Archives, 11945, in Kinkor, "Whydah Sourcebook," 118.

226. "111. Deposition of Ralph Merry and Samuel Roberts," in Jameson, *Privateering and Piracy in the Colonial Period*, 301–2.

227. Clifford and Perry, *Expedition Whydah*, 260–64.

228. Ibid., 265.

229. "107. Cyprian Southack to Governor Samuel Shute, [5?] May 1717," in Jameson, *Privateering and Piracy in the Colonial Period*, 291–92; "Cyprian Southack to Governor Shute, Eastham, 8 May 1717," Massachusetts Archives 51:289, 289a, in Kinkor, "Whydah Sourcebook," 127; "Eastham 9 May 1717: Thirdsday at Pirate Wreck," Journal of Cyprian Southack, in Kinkor, "Whydah Sourcebook," 129.

230. Julian is believed to be from the region of Nicaragua and Honduras in Central America called the Costa de Miskitos.

231. "Advertisement by Cyprian Southack, Eastham, 6 May 1717," Massachusetts Archives 63:249, in Kinkor, "Whydah Sourcebook," 126.

232. "Cyprian Southack to Governor Shute," in Kinkor, "Whydah Sourcebook," 114–15.

233. "Royal Instructions: Disposal of Pirates' Goods," Labaree, 1935: #649 (1:453), in Kinkor, "Whydah Sourcebook," 93.

234. "Boston Advertisement of 17 June 1717," *Boston News-Letter*, in Kinkor, "Whydah Sourcebook," 160.

235. "Boston Advertisement of 22 July 1717," *Boston News-Letter*, in Kinkor, "Whydah Sourcebook," 167.

236. Woodard, *Republic of Pirates*, 193.

237. *Trials of eight persons indited for piracy*, 13.

238. Ibid., 13–15.

239. *Compos Mentis* refers to "someone of sound mind."

240. Mather, *Instructions to the living*, 37–38.

Part V

241. Horn, "Recipients."
242. Mather, *Instructions to the living*, 5–7.
243. Ibid., 10–19.
244. Ibid., 20–27, 38.
245. Brunelle, *Bellamy's Bride*, 31–32.
246. Ibid., 35–36.
247. Ibid., 36. You can learn the entire twists, turns, and versions of Maria Hallett's story in Brunelle's *Bellamy's Bride*.
248. Clifford and Perry, *Expedition Whydah*, 293–94.
249. Ibid., 309.

BIBLIOGRAPHY

Books

Beal, Clifford. *Quelch's Gold: Piracy, Greed, and Betrayal in Colonial New England.* Washington, D.C.: Potomac Books, Inc., 2008.

Brunelle, Kathleen. *Bellamy's Bride: The Search for Maria Hallett of Cape Cod.* Charleston, SC: The History Press, 2010.

Cheney, C.R., and Michael Jones, eds. *A Handbook of Dates: For Students of English History.* 4th ed. Cambridge, UK: Cambridge University Press, 2000.

Clifford, Barry, and Paul Perry. *Expedition Whydah: The Story of the World's First Excavation of a Pirate Treasure Ship and the Man Who Found Her.* New York: Cliff Street Books, 1999.

Clodfelter, Micheal. *Warfare and Armed Conflicts: A Statistical Reference to Casualty and Other Figures 1500–2000.* Jefferson, NC: McFarland & Company, Inc., 1992.

Dolin, Eric Jay. *Black Flags, Blue Waters: The Epic History of America's Most Notorious Pirates.* New York: Liveright Publishing Corporation, 2018.

Dow, George Francis, and John Henry Edmonds. *The Pirates of the New England Coast, 1630–1730.* New York: Dover Publications, Inc., 1996.

Gardner, John. *Grendel.* New York: Vintage Books, 1989.

Hanna, Mark G. *Pirate Nests and the Rise of the British Empire, 1570–1740.* Chapel Hill: University of North Carolina Press, 2015.

Harris, Tim. *Restoration: Charles II and His Kingdoms, 1660–1685.* London: Penguin Books, 2006.

Johnson, Emory R., T.W. Van Metre, Grover G. Huebner, and David Scott Hanchett. *History of Domestic and Foreign Commerce of the United States*. Washington, D.C.: Carnegie Institution of Washington, 1915.

Konstam, Angus. *The History of Pirates*. Guilford, CT: Lyons Press, 2002.

McCusker, John J. "British Colonial Exchange on London: The North American Colonies." In *Money and Exchange in Europe and America, 1600–1775: A Handbook*, 116–233. Chapel Hill: University of North Carolina Press, 1978. www.jstor.org/stable/10.5149/9780807839423_mccusker.6.

Ogg, David. *England in the Reign of Charles II*. Vol. 1. 2 vols. Oxford, UK: Clarendon Press, 1934.

Pavese, Cesare. *This Business of Living: Diaries, 1935–1950*. Rev. ed. Oxfordshire, UK: Routledge, 2017.

Rediker, Marcus. *Villains of All Nations: Atlantic Pirates in the Golden Age*. Boston: Beacon Press, 2005.

Selinger, Gail. *Pirates of New England: Ruthless Raiders and Rotten Renegades*. Guilford, CT: Globe Pequot, 2017.

Washburn, Emory. *Sketches of the Judicial History of Massachusetts: From 1630 to the Revolution in 1775*. Boston: Charles C. Little and James Brown, 1840. www.google.com/books/edition/Sketches_of_the_Judicial_History_of_Mass/gpssAAAAIAAJ?hl=en&gbpv=0.

Woodard, Colin. *The Republic of Pirates: Being the True and Surprising Story of the Caribbean Pirates and the Man Who Brought Them Down*. New York: Harcourt, Inc., 2007.

Journal Articles

Boxer, C.R. "Some Second Thoughts on the Third Anglo-Dutch War, 1672–1674." *Transactions of the Royal Historical Society* 19 (1969): 67–94. doi.org/10.2307/3678740.

Cave, Alfred A. "Who Killed John Stone? A Note on the Origins of the Pequot War." *William and Mary Quarterly* 49, no. 3 (July 1992): 509–21. doi.org/10.2307/2947109.

Clark, Gregory. "Farm Wages and Living Standards in the Industrial Revolution: England, 1670–1869." *Economic History Review* 54, no. 3 (August 2001): 477–505. doi.org/10.1111/1468-0289.00200.

Hutton, Ronald. "The Making of the Secret Treaty of Dover, 1668–1670." *Historical Journal* 29, no. 2 (1986): 297–318. doi.org/10.1017/s0018246x00018756.

Published Primary Sources

An Account of the Behaviour and Last Dying Speeches of the Six Pirates, That Were Executed on Charles River, Boston Side on Fryday June 30th 1704. Viz. Capt. John Quelch, John Lambert, Christopher Scudamore, John Miller, Erasmus Peterson and Peter Roach. Boston: Nicholas Boone, 1704. www.loc.gov/resource/ rbpe.03303400.

Acts and Ordinances of the Interregnum, 1642–1660. Edited by C.H. Firth and R.S. Rait. London: His Majesty's Stationery Office, 1911. British History Online. www.british-history.ac.uk/no-series/acts-ordinances-interregnum.

Ames, Ellis, Abner Cheney Goodell, John Henry Clifford, Alexander Strong Wheeler, William Cross Williamson, and Melville Madison Bigelow, eds. *The Acts and Resolves, Public and Private, of the Province of the Massachusetts Bay: To Which Are Prefixed the Charters of the Province, with Historical and Explanatory Notes.* Vol. 8. Boston: Wright & Potter Printing Co., 1869. www.google. com/books/edition/The_Acts_and_Resolves_Public_and_Private/e_ jRKBiXYegC?hl=en&gbpv=0.

B–, J–. "A Letter to a Member of Parliament concerning the Suppression of Piracy, 20 March 1699." Ann Arbor, MI: Early English Books Online Text Creation Partnership, 2011. name.umdl.umich.edu/B08403.0001.001

Calendar of State Papers, Colonial, America and West Indies: Volumes 1–41, 1574–1739. Edited by W. Noel Sainsbury and J.W. Fortescue. London: Her Majesty's Stationery Office, 1896. British History Online. www.british-history.ac.uk/ search/series/cal-state-papers--colonial--america-west-indies.

Calendar of State Papers Relating to English Affairs in the Archives of Venice, Volume 10, 1603–1607. Edited by Horatio F. Brown. London: Her Majesty's Stationery Office, 1900. British History Online. www.british-history. ac.uk/cal-state-papers/venice/vol10.

Calendar of the Cecil Papers in Hatfield House: Volume 18, 1606. Edited by M.S. Giuseppi. London: His Majesty's Stationery Office, 1940. British History Online. www.british-history.ac.uk/cal-cecil-papers/vol18.

Calendar of the Cecil Papers in Hatfield House: Volume 20, 1608. Edited by M.S. Giuseppi and G. Dyfnallt Owen. London: Her Majesty's Stationery Office, 1968. British History Online. www.british-history.ac.uk/cal-cecil-papers/vol20.

Clap, Roger. *Memoirs of Capt. Roger Clap. Relating some of God's remarkable providences to him, in bringing him into New-England…* Edited by Thomas Prince and James Blake. Boston: B. Green, 1731; Ann Arbor, MI: Early English

Books Online Text Creation Partnership, 2011. name.umdl.umich.edu/N02849.0001.001.

Crowell, Robert, and David Choate. *History of the Town of Essex from 1634 to 1868*. Springfield, MA: Press of Samuel Bowles & Co., 1868. www.google.com/books/edition/History_of_the_Town_of_Essex/DF_GPpZU75EC?hl=en&gbpv=0.

Dow, George Francis, ed. *Records and Files of the Quarterly Courts of Essex County, Massachusetts: 1636–1656*. Vol. 1. Salem, MA: Essex Institute, 1911. www.google.com/books/edition/Records_and_Files_of_the_Quarterly_Court/gy01AQAAMAAJ?hl=en&gbpv=0.

Dudley, Joseph. *The Arraignment, Tryal, and Condemnation of Capt. John Quelch: And Others of His Company, &c. for Sundry Piracies, Robberies, and Murder, Committed upon the Subjects of the King of Portugal, Her Majesty's Allie, on the Coast of Brasil, &c...* London: Printed for Benjamin Bragg in Avemary-Lane, 1705. PDF.

Hawkins, Sir Richard. *The Observations of Sir Richard Hawkins, Knt in His Voyage into the South Sea in the Year 1593, Reprinted from the Edition of 1622*. Edited by C.R. Drinkwater Bethune. London: Hakluyt Society, 1847. www.gutenberg.org/files/57502/57502-h/57502-h.htm.

Hutchinson, Thomas. *The History of the Colony of Massachuset's Bay, from the First Settlement Thereof in 1628, Until Its Incorporation with the Colony of Plimouth, Province of Main, &c. by the Charter of King William and Queen Mary in 1691*. 2nd ed. London: M. Richardson, 1765. www.google.com/books/edition/_/nMQUAAAAQAAJ?hl=en&gbpv=0.

James I, King of England. *By the King. A proclamation against pirats*. London: By the deputies of Robert Barker, 1609; Ann Arbor, MI: Early English Books Online Text Creation Partnership, 2011. name.umdl.umich.edu/A69345.0001.001.

Jameson, John Franklin, ed. *Privateering and Piracy in the Colonial Period: Illustrative Documents*. New York: Macmillan Company, 1923. www.gutenberg.org/files/24882/24882-h/24882-h.htm.

Johnson, Captain Charles. *The History of the Pyrates: Containing the Lives of Captain Misson, Captain Bowen, Captain Kidd, Captain Tew, Captain Halsey, Captain White, Captain Condent, Captain Bellamy, Captain Fly, Captain Howard, Captain Lewis, Captain Cornelius, Captain Williams, Captain Burgess, Captain North, and Their Several Crews*. Vol. 2. London: T. Woodward. www.gutenberg.org/files/57005/57005-h/57005-h.htm.

Kingsbury, Susan Myra, ed. *Records of the Virginia Company of London, 1622–24: The Court Book, from the Manuscript in the Library of Congress*. Vol. 1. 2

vols. Washington, D.C.: Government Printing Office, 1906. lccn.loc. gov/06035006.

Mather, Reverend Cotton. *Instructions to the living, from the condition of the dead. A brief relation of remarkables in the shipwreck of above one hundred pirates, who were cast away in the ship Whido, on the coast of New-England, April 26. 1717…* Boston: John Allen, 1717; Ann Arbor, MI: Early English Books Online Text Creation Partnership, 2011. name.umdl.umich.edu/N01600.0001.001.

Niles, Samuel. "The French on Block Island." In *A Library of American Literature: From the Earliest Settlement to the Present Time.* Vol. 2: 1–16. Edited by Edmund Clarence Stedman and Ellen Mackay Hutchinson. New York: Charles L. Webster & Company, 1891. www.bartleby.com/400/prose/327.html.

Roberts, Richard Arthur, ed. *Calendar of the Manuscripts of the Most Hon. the Marquis of Salisbury, K.G.* Vol. 8. London: Mackie & Co., LD., 1899. www.google.com/books/edition/Calendar_of_the_Manuscripts_of_the_Most/d78KAAAAYAAJ?hl=en&gbpv=0.

Seneca, Lucius Annaeus. *Ad Lucilium Epistulae Morales: With an English Translation.* Translated by Richard M. Gummere. Vol. 1. 3 vols. London: William Heinemann, 1917. www.google.com/books/edition/Ad_Lucilium_Epistulae_Morales/H3w6AQAAMAAJ?hl=en&gbpv=0.

"Seneca ('the Younger') c.4 BC–AD 65." In *The Oxford Dictionary of Quotations*, edited by Elizabeth Knowles. 8th ed. Oxford: Oxford University Press, Inc., 2014. ezproxy.snhu.edu/login?url=https://search.credoreference.com/content/entry/oupoq/seneca_the_younger_c_4_bc_ad_65/0?institutionId=943.

Smith, John. *The True Travels, Adventures, and Observations of Captain John Smith into Europe, Asia, Africa, and America: From Ann. Dom. 1593 to 1629.* Edited by Roger Burch. Project Gutenberg. London, 1630. www.gutenberg.org/cache/epub/55199/pg55199-images.html.

Statutes of the Realm. Vol. 5, *1628–80.* Edited by John Raithby. s.l.: Great Britain Record Commission 1819, British History Online. www.british-history.ac.uk/statutes-realm/vol5.

Statutes of the Realm. Vol. 7, *1695–1701.* Edited by John Raithby. s.l.: Great Britain Record Commission 1820. British History Online. www.british-history.ac.uk/statutes-realm/vol7.

St. Clair, Henry. *The Criminal Calendar, or an Awful Warning to the Youth of America; Being an Account of the Most Notorious Pirates, Highwaymen and Other Malefactors Who Have Figured in This Hemisphere.* Frederic S. Hill, 1831.

The Trials of eight persons indited for piracy &c. Of whom two were acquitted, and the rest found guilty. At a justiciary Court of Admiralty assembled and held in Boston within His Majesty's province of the Massachusetts-Bay in New-England, on the 18th of October 1717... Boston: B. Green, 1718; Ann Arbor, MI: Early English Books Online Text Creation Partnership, 2011. quod.lib.umich.edu/e/evans/N01688.0001.001?rgn=main;view=fulltext.

Underhill, John. *Nevves from America; or, a New and Experimentall Discoverie of New England...* Edited by Paul Royster. London: Printed by J. Dawson for Peter Cole, 1638. digitalcommons.unl.edu/etas/37.

Whitehead, William A., ed. *Documents Relating to the Colonial History of the State of New Jersey, 1687–1703.* Vol. 2. Newark, NJ: Daily Advertiser Printing House, 1881.

Winthrop, John. *Winthrop's Journal: History of New England, 1630–1649.* Edited by James Kendall Hosmer. Vol. 1. New York: Charles Scribner's Sons, 1908. marbleheadmuseum.org/wp-content/uploads/2021/01/pp-187-260-331Winthrop_s_Journal_History_of_New_Englan.pdf.

Archival Sources

Bradford, William. *Bradford's History "Of Plimoth Plantation" from the Original Manuscript: with a Report of the Proceedings Incident to the Return of the Manuscript to Massachusetts,* 1897. Manuscripts Collection. Non-Governmental and Special Collections, State Library of Massachusetts, Boston. archives.lib.state.ma.us/2452/208249.

Felt, Reverend Joseph, comp. Massachusetts Archives Collection: Military, 1712–1747. Vol. 72. 328 vols. Boston, 1830.

Unpublished Primary Sources

Kinkor, Kenneth J., ed. "The Whydah Sourcebook (2003)." Unpublished volume received through private correspondence.

Web Sources

Böhne, Matthias, and Olaf Simons. "The Marteau Early 18ᵗʰ-Century Currency Converter." Pierre Marteau Virtual Publishers, 2004. www.pierre-marteau.com/currency/converter/fra-eng.html.

Ferris, John P., and Paul Hunneyball. "HAWKINS, Sir Richard (C. 1560–1622), of Plymouth, Devon." The History of Parliament Online. Cambridge University Press. www.historyofparliamentonline.org/volume/1604-1629/member/hawkins-sir-richard-1560-1622.

Horn, Dara. "The Recipients." Interview by Julia DeWitt. *Snap Judgement*, NPR, May 22, 2015. Transcript. www.npr.org/2015/05/22/408764802/the-recipients.

Maugh, Thomas H., II. "A Pirate's Life for Him—at Age 9." *Los Angeles Times*, June 1, 2006. www.latimes.com/archives/la-xpm-2006-jun-01-sci-pirate1-story.html.

Nye, Eric W. "Pounds Sterling to Dollars: Historical Conversion of Currency." www.uwyo.edu/numimage/currency.htm.

INDEX

A

Aernouts, Jurriaen 56, 60
Agnes 17, 110
Amity 73
Anne Galley 110, 114

B

Baker, Thomas 103, 118, 119, 123
Beer, Captain 17, 109
Bonetta 17, 103
Brown, John 102, 111, 114, 118,
        119, 124
Bull, Dixie 37, 39, 42

C

Cape Cod 15, 93, 95, 112, 114,
        116
Caverley, Richard 103, 110
Cromwell, Oliver 49, 52
Cromwell, Thomas 46, 48

D

Davis, Thomas 105, 116, 119

E

Elizabethan sea dogs 18, 24
Endeavor 110
English Civil War 33, 42, 46, 49
Every, Henry 75

F

Fisher 112, 114
Flying Gang 98, 102
Flying Horse 55, 56

G

Glorious Revolution 49, 66, 69

H

Hallett, Maria 15, 93, 112, 125
Hispaniola 52, 107, 108

Hoof, Peter Cornelius 98, 104, 118, 119, 124
Hornigold, Benjamin 100, 102
Hull, Edward 50
Hull, John 50

J

Jackson, William 42, 46, 48
Jamaica 46, 52, 55, 59, 61, 64, 103, 105, 107
Jennings, Henry 98
Julian, John 116, 118

K

King, John 104
King William's War 69

L

La Buse. *See* Levasseur, Olivier
Levasseur, Olivier 102, 103, 105

M

Madagascar 71, 79
Marianne 100, 102, 105, 107, 109, 110
Mary Anne 17, 112, 114, 117
Mather, Cotton 119, 123

P

Paine, Thomas 64, 70, 96
Pearl 105
Pequot War 41, 42
Postillion 102

Q

Queen Anne's War 81
Quelch, John 81, 82, 84, 89
Quintor, Hendrick 102, 118, 119

R

Rhoades, John 56
Rich, Sir Robert 31, 42, 46, 48

S

Shuan, John 109, 118, 119
Southack, Cyprian 116
St. Marie 100
Stone, John 40, 41
Sultana, The 105, 107

T

Tanner Frigate 108
Tew, Thomas 72, 73

V

Van Vorst, Simon 103, 112, 118, 119, 124

W

Warwick, Earl of. *See* Rich, Sir Robert
West Indies 40, 42, 46, 48, 50, 52, 83, 111
Whydah 12, 15, 104, 106, 108, 110, 114, 116, 123, 126
Winthrop, John 38, 39, 43, 46

ABOUT THE AUTHOR

Jamie L.H. Goodall, PhD, is a historian with the U.S. Army Center of Military History in Washington, D.C. She has a PhD in history from The Ohio State University, with specializations in Atlantic world, early American, and military histories. She is also a first-generation college student. Goodall is an expert on golden age piracy and has published with outlets like The History Press, the *Washington Post*, and *National Geographic*. She lives in Northern Virginia with her partner, Kyle, and her Boxers, Thomas Jefferson and John Tyler. When she's not researching, writing, or reading, she enjoys getting tattoos, eating cheese, and pretending to know a lot about wine. You can find her and her #SwashbucklinStoryTime on Twitter: @L_Historienne.

Notice: The views expressed in this manuscript are the author's and do not reflect those of the U.S. Army Center of Military History, the U.S. Army, or the Department of Defense.